To

ACCELERATION

9 Secrets to Achieving
Maximum Success in Minimum Time

By ZENZO MATOGA

Copyright © 2014 by Zenzo Matoga

Acceleration
9 Secrets to Achieving Maximum Success in Minimum Time
by Zenzo Matoga

Printed in the United States of America

ISBN 9781498410243

All rights reserved solely by the author. The author guarantees all contents are original and do not infringe upon the legal rights of any other person or work. No part of this book may be reproduced in any form without the permission of the author. The views expressed in this book are not necessarily those of the publisher.

Scripture quotations taken from The Holy Bible, New International Version (NIV). Copyright © 1973, 1978, 1984, 2011 by Biblica, Inc.™. Used by permission. All rights reserved.

The New King James Version (NKJV). Copyright © 1982 by Thomas Nelson, Inc. Used by permission. All rights reserved.

The King James Version (KJV) – *public domain.*

The Amplified Bible (AMP). Copyright © 1954, 1958, 1962, 1964, 1965, 1987 by The Lockman Foundation. Used by permission. All rights reserved.

The Message (MSG). Copyright © 1993, 1994, 1995, 1996, 2000, 2001, 2002. Used by permission of NavPress Publishing Group. Used by permission. All rights reserved.

CONTENTS

FOREWORD

As Mike and I sat across the breakfast table from the next generation leader, Zenzo Matoga, we quickly realized the Malawian-born leader was meant to shape the future of both our nation and the nations of the world.

Zenzo had already mobilized large gatherings for worship and prayer under the shadow of Harvard University. Perhaps this is an answer of many believers' cries to return this country to the dreams of its godly founders.

We noted his keen mind as he shared the legacy from his father of both a scientific mind and a preacher's passion for God. His mother's character and love of prayer as a woman of God formed before our eyes as he poured out to us his vision for New England to return to its godly roots. It is such a wondrous blessing to see how the sons and daughters of former missions' movements are flowing back to America to return zeal to the land. How like God to use an African-born American to wake up the land of the birthplace of freedom.

At that special breakfast, on the river and in the city where the Boston Tea Party took place, we sensed that Zenzo needed to write this book. There is no doubt that it will be the first of many to come.

This is a remarkable book! Though short, every page is packed with keys to maximize one's time. What necessary lessons! I can see that the man we first came to know as a man of prayer is both left and right-brained. He also is a diligent student to improve time management. After reading the secrets of developing leadership character, building teams, choosing a partner to achieve success, understanding timing, and many other rich keys, you will be changed.

Many people start out with good intentions for success. Others desire to build a dream team to see their visions come to reality and fruition; yet, many fall by the wayside of only having a good idea. In my opinion, many lack the skill-set to be an implementer of those good ideas, and others simply don't want to work hard to make it happen.

I believe many will read this book and see the Acceleration they have longed for in their personal lives, families, ministries, and careers.

Prepare to be changed!

Many blessings!

Cindy Jacobs
Generals International
Dallas, Texas

DEDICATION

I dedicate this book, my first book, to my dear parents,

Bishop Geoffrey and Pastor Barbara Matoga.

You are forever my heroes!

Everything I am today is because of you.

ACKNOWLEDGEMENTS

Special thanks:
To my best friend and lovely bride of 8 years, Michelle,
for the outstanding job editing this book,
for being the perfect helpmate and the best partner in life;

To my apostolic covering, Bishop Gideon
and Pastor Yvonne Thompson;

To my pastors, Pastor Matthew and Mona Thompson,
and the entire Jubilee church family;

To the UNOW executive leadership team for believing
in the vision God put in Michelle and I;

To my dear mentor and friend Bob Weiner

INTRODUCTION

ACCELERATION

9 Secrets to Achieving Maximum Success in Minimum Time

If you had a choice, would you travel the journey to your destiny on a bicycle or a Mercedes Benz? It's a no-brainer... I'm sure, just like me, you would rather get to your destiny driving a Mercedes, not on a BMX bike. The Benz is not only faster, but safer, more efficient, more comfortable and more reliable than a bike. There is always a faster and more efficient way to get something done. Getting things done efficiently and at an accelerated rate allows you to have maximum impact and influence. Whereas, getting stuck on unfinished projects not only frustrates you, but holds you back from releasing your purpose, and ultimately from finding solutions to the world's problems.

Ephesians 5:15-16 (New King James Version)
See then that you walk circumspectly, not as fools but as wise, redeeming the time, because the days are evil.

Ephesians 5:15-16 (Amplified Version)
Look carefully then how you walk! Live purposefully and worthily and accurately, not as the unwise and witless, but as wise (sensible, intelligent people), Making the very most of the time [buying up each opportunity], because the days are evil.

In this scripture, Paul is instructing the people to walk wisely and redeem time for the days are evil. In other words, Paul was saying that the way to counterattack evil is to make the very most of time and accomplish your God-given purpose at an accelerated rate. You have to know that every day you delay to fulfill your God-given mission is yet another gift handed to the enemy to fulfill evil. Yet, on the other hand, when you fulfill your God-given mission at an accelerated level, you interrupt the enemy's mission like the police have just walked into a robbery. I'm more interested in stopping the enemy from robbing what I have than to let him steal and then have to take back what he has stolen from me. It's the acceleration of good that diminishes evil. Edmund Burke said, "The only thing necessary for the triumph of evil is for good men to do nothing."

I've found that disobedience will also slow down acceleration. God gave the children of Israel a promise to deliver them from captivity in Egypt and bring them to the Promised Land in Canaan. The trip from Egypt to Canaan was only supposed to take them 11 days. Because of their mistakes, disobedience, lack of vision and strategy, it took them 40 years! On top of that, only two people out of millions made it into the Promised Land (Deuteronomy 1, Joshua 1). This story teaches us that if poor decisions and unnecessary mistakes can delay your destiny, then wise counsel, great vision and total obedience to God's laws and principles can accelerate it. In this book we will discuss 9 Biblical and time-tested principles that will give you acceleration (God's speed) in everything you set your mind to do.

You were Created for Acceleration

James 1:17 "Every good and perfect gift is from above, coming down from the Father of the heavenly lights, who does not change like shifting shadows."

1 John 1:15 "This is the message we have heard from him and declare to you: God is light; in him there is no darkness at all."

God is light! The book of James describes God as the father of lights! And the first thing God created on day one of creation was light! Light stands for several things: knowledge, revelation, illumination, purpose, etc. Light came in the beginning and it dispersed darkness: ignorance, purposelessness, no direction, no identity, void, evil. But light also represents speed (Acceleration!). Modern physics has proven that light is the fastest thing on earth. Its velocity is about 186,282.397 miles per second. That means that if you traveled around the Earth's equator at the speed of light, you would travel around the entire planet 7.4 times in approximately one second! Light is fast. Light represents acceleration.

When scripture says "God is light," it's not only implying that He is wise and all-knowing, but we are also being introduced to God's nature and one of His attributes — acceleration. God is the one who created the cheetah with his speed of 70 mph (110 kmh) and ability to accelerate from walking speed to about 40 mph (65 kmh) in less than two seconds. He gave wisdom to the one who made the Bugatti Veyron, the fastest car in the world with a top speed of 268 miles per hour. He also gave wisdom to the one who made the Lockheed SR-71 "Blackbird," the fastest jet in the world. Speed is one of God's attributes! It's a part of His divine DNA! Remember, He created us in His image. The same image of light! Speed! Acceleration! That's why we all like fast things. Whether it's a fast phone signal, or a fast processing computer, or simply watching a good race car show, we all have the proclivity to speed and acceleration. Isn't it fascinating that no one teaches little kids to race... they just get up and do it out of instinct as soon as they can run. We were created in the image of God!

Chapter 1

VISION

My Definition of Vision

C lear mental pictures derived out of your passion, conviction, and purpose that you can follow and others can follow with you.

I know it's a complex definition, but I will break it down for you. Here is a simple definition: Vision is the power to see the future.

There are 3 Stages in the Process of Vision Creation
Passion-Purpose-Vision

1) Your passion and conviction reveals your purpose.
2) Your purpose then determines your vision.
3) Your vision draws you and others to follow.

Everyone has passion and conviction, but few know how to translate these emotions into a tangible and descriptive blueprint. Next, I will help you to discover these areas in your life and how to create a vision with them.

1. Passion

Everyone is passionate about something. There is something that makes you the most excited. There is a desire in all of us to accomplish something. For some it's acquiring certain levels of education, for others it's innovating, or it could be simply having a great family. While for others it's traveling the whole world. Ultimately, what you are passionate about leads you in the direction of discovering what your purpose is in life. Don't worry, I will break this down and elaborate some more for you. Today you will be able to know how to discover your purpose in life.

Another form of passion is conviction. It's passion working in the opposite direction. It's the desire to solve issues in our world. For some, it's their conviction that reveals their purpose in life. There is something that breaks your heart or simply annoys you so much you can't go on in life until you fix it. Your passion and conviction lead you to your purpose in life.

How do I discover my passion? Ask yourself these 4 questions:

1) If I did not have to work to survive; if I had all the money in the world, what would still make me excited to wake up in the morning and do for the rest of my life?
2) What breaks my heart the most in this world that I would like to solve?
3) What do I enjoy so much that I don't even care about time when I'm doing it?
4) What comes easy for me? I can accomplish this great work and enjoy doing it at the same time.

Your answers to these questions will help you discover your greatest passion and conviction. This is what leads you to discovering your purpose in life.

2. Purpose

The purpose of my pencil is to solve a writing problem.
The purpose of my car is to solve a transportation problem.
The purpose of my phone is to solve a communication problem.
The purpose of a doctor is to solve a sickness problem.

The purpose of a lawyer is to solve legal problems.
The purpose of a teacher is to solve an ignorance problem.

Everything and everyone was created with a purpose. You were created to provide solutions for something and someone, but it's your passion and conviction that causes you to realize the primary problem you were born to solve in life—your purpose. Passion and conviction comes first, and then purpose, then a vision is birthed out of your purpose in life.

3. Vision

Now, when you discover what your purpose is in life by following your passion or conviction, you have to find the vehicle that will put substance to it all—vision. You have to paint a clear picture and turn your feelings into something tangible.

Henry Ford discovered his passion for engines and his purpose to solve the transportation problem, so he started working on drawings to improve the car. He had a vision for a Ford automobile.

Thomas Edison discovered his passion for electronics and also his obsession to create light and fix the problem of darkness in the home. He started making sketches in attempt to make a light bulb. He had a vision to create a bulb.

People Only Follow Vision

People around you may be inspired by your passion and conviction, but they won't follow you because of that, they follow vision—something tangible. You have to have a set of ideas that communicate what you feel and see. You don't vote for a mayor just because he or she is passionate about changing your city, or because they believe that's their purpose in life. You only vote when you are convinced that they have a great vision (manifesto/great ideas that will make a difference). That's why the Bible says, "Without a vision the people perish" (Prov. 29:18). People follow vision, not someone with just a great heart. But a great vision is birthed out of a person who has understood what their purpose is in life—the problem they were born to solve and provide solutions for.

Michelangelo was passionate about art. His purpose was to touch people with his pictures and paintings. He had a vision for the Sistine Chapel.

Oprah was passionate about reading, public speaking, and teaching from a tender age. She discovered her purpose to educate and change people through information. The tangible vision for Harpo Studios was birthed out of this. The studio was the vehicle for her passion and purpose.

Abraham Lincoln had a conviction that slavery was wrong. He discovered that "bringing justice through politics" was his purpose in life, and announced his clear and methodical vision to abolish slavery.

8 Benefits of Vision

1. Gives You Speed

The sooner you know the direction, the sooner you start, and the quicker you travel. In the Bible, Habakkuk 2:2 says, "Write the vision and make it plain on tablets, that he may RUN who reads it." The word "run" connotes speed. Most super successful people knew what they wanted to do early on in life. Ninety percent of unsuccessful people never knew what they wanted to do and lost valuable time experimenting with their lives. Vision accelerates you and the lack of it slows you down.

2. Focus

Without having an intended and measurable goal (vision), others can easily divert you and lead you off to something else of less significance. Vision keeps you focused. Vision puts your priorities in order. A magnifying glass has the power to burn a hole through a piece of paper when it's held up to the sun and focused on a single point long enough. Having laser focus is the secret to success. A great leader pays a great price by saying "NO" numerous times to things that are good, but not in line with their vision and purpose. The clearer the vision, the greater the focus. That's why you have to write it down. Read it every day. Lack of vision is the reason you are not able to focus and become great at one thing. When you get a strong and clear vision it demands your attention. A great vision consumes you.

3. High Productivity

Steve Jobs, Michael Jordan, and Michelangelo all focused on one thing and they became masters in their field. They concentrated their time and efforts on one thing. Whatever you spend your time and concentration on, you become a master of. Repetition produces consistency, and consistency produces efficiency. Efficiency means you achieve great quality and quantity in a short time.

4. Management of Resources

"For which of you, intending to build a tower, does not sit down first and count the cost, whether he has enough to finish it—lest, after he has laid the foundation, and is not able to finish, all who see it begin to mock him, saying, 'This man began to build and was not able to finish'" (Luke 14:28-30). You can easily waste your valuable resources on the lesser when you don't have a clear vision of your expected end. Vision helps you to be an excellent steward of your resources: time, treasure and talent.

5. Makes You Effective

Not every productive person is effective. Productivity is simply the ability to get things done, while effectiveness is solving problems and meeting the intended goal with your productivity. Are you getting a lot of things done but not changing much at all? It might be time to get a stronger vision. A great vision makes you effective. Study the story of any great visionary and you will discover highly effective people—people who made, and are making, a difference!

6. Attracts People

People are attracted and remain inspired when a great vision is in place. Leaders who have to control and manipulate lack vision. You don't have to rule with an iron fist when you have a great vision in place. People will commit their lives when they have found a great cause to live for. Vision keeps people motivated. Nehemiah had a vision to rebuild the walls of Jerusalem. It was a noble cause for his people. They were drawn and united around this great cause, and despite major opposition, the walls were rebuilt.

7. Creates Legacy

A great vision outlives the visionary. When a great vision that has consumed people is in place, it does not die when the visionary dies. Martin Luther King Jr.'s dream for a non-segregated America was not killed when he was killed. Abe Lincoln's dream for a slave-free America did not die when he was assassinated. Their visions started revolutions among the people. They could not destroy the vision even though they managed to destroy the visionaries. When your vision is birthed out of a great passion and conviction, it carries a life of its own and is unstoppable.

8. Communicates Expectations

Without clear expectations, chaos comes in quickly. I've found that unmet expectations, whether from the leader/visionary or from those under the visionary, is one of the greatest causes of conflict. A great vision should also include statements that communicate clear expectations for those running with it.

How to Execute Vision: 3 Steps You Must Follow in Order to Effectively Accomplish Your Vision

GOALS-STEPS-TASKS-VISION

A vision without clear goals, steps and tasks is useless. Yes, I really mean that—useless. You need to have a systematic plan to reach your vision. Without clear goals, steps and tasks, a vision is reduced to being merely a signpost. Reading a signpost does not take you to your destination until you follow the directions.

Example

Vision: Let's say your vision is to be healthy and lose 60 pounds in 6 months. (A great vision should always have a specific timeline.)

Goals: Your goal can be to lose 20 pounds every 2 months, which means you have three goals: 1) To lose 20 pounds in 2 months; 2) lose 40 pounds in 4 months; and 3) lose 60 pounds in 6 months. You have three short-term goals which lead you to accomplishing your vision.

Steps: Next, you have to decide the steps you are going to take in order to accomplish your short-term goals. You can say, "I will work out 3 times every week in order to lose 20 pounds in 2 months (8 weeks)." Create a schedule and say, "I will work out on Mondays, Tuesdays, and Fridays." Now you have given yourself clear steps to lead you to be successful in accomplishing your intended short-term goals.

Tasks: Finally, you need specific tasks that will lead you to fulfill your steps. You can say to yourself, "In order for me to be successful in my steps (working out 3 times per week), I'm going to have a trainer write out specific workouts for my body for each day I'm in the gym: arms and chest on Mondays, legs and back on Tuesdays, and cardio on Fridays."

Without these clear goals, steps and tasks leading you to your vision, you will not be anywhere close to accomplishing your vision of losing 60 pounds in 6 months. Your calendar and schedule should serve the goals, steps and tasks for your vision to be reached. The good news is that even if you fall a little short, as long as you are diligently doing your part, you will be closer to where you need to be.

Key Questions
1. What's the one most important thing I have to accomplish in my lifetime?
2. What are the goals, steps and tasks I need to take to get there?
3. What should I do every week to keep me inspired and passionate about my vision?

Chapter 2

TRUST

"High trust organizations outperform low trust organizations by 286 percent in total return to shareholders."

Watson Wyatt/Human Capital Study

There is a secret of acceleration in the principle of TRUST. Trust is an asset that speeds up your personal growth and the growth of your organization. It increases your equity, authenticity, and credibility—inwardly and outwardly. At the end of the day, what really matters is that people trust you as an individual first and then they also trust your product, vision, and organization. Yes, it sounds simple and yet I have found that very few people know how to cultivate trust and use it as a speed accelerator. Without building trust on a personal level and in an organization, you will always find yourself taking three steps forward and four steps backwards. Though many people claim to know what trust is, very few really know what it means in depth or in action. Few know how to establish trust and sustain it. Trust is the secret to every high achiever. Trust is a major asset and the lack of it, a major liability.

If one were to ask me the distinction between people, marriages, ministries and organizations that are successful and moving full speed ahead versus those that are stagnant, I would unequivocally say the difference is found in whether or not there is trust on a personal level and in the culture of their organization. It's that simple: no trust, no speed. More trust, more speed.

7 Ways Lack of Trust Stops Acceleration

1. No Collaboration

Without trust there is no collaboration. Collaboration is the "master plan" formed out of the collective strategies from individual team members. Steve Jobs and his partner Steve Wozniack were able to propel Apple into one of the best brands in the world because of their collaboration (combined strategies). When there is no trust, people hold back their strategies and ideas. There is no collaboration. And no collaboration means there is no ground-breaking and cutting edge ideas that release acceleration.

2. No Synergy

Synergy is the energy, the enthusiasm, the fire, and passion that is derived out of a group of like-minded people working together. I must say that there is a distinction between synergy and collaboration. While collaboration is teamwork, synergy is the energy and fuel you get from the encouragement and motivation of a great team. When people don't trust you, they hold back from working with you. When people don't trust each other, it's difficult for them to work together. Because of this lack of trust, everybody puts up walls to preserve and protect themselves, and these walls end up blocking and stopping synergy.

3. Minimal Productivity

Without collaboration and synergy, productivity automatically suffers. When people don't work together and resolve to hiding in their own corners, productivity slows down. Everyone becomes consumed with protecting themselves instead of working and building.

4. More Conflicts

An atmosphere where people don't trust each other quickly becomes a conflict-infested zone. Small issues are magnified and conflicts increase. People end up wasting time managing conflicts and solving disputes instead of getting the job done, once again thwarting growth and killing productivity. Marriages that have experienced infidelity become a high conflict zone because the trust level drops significantly.

5. Poor Communication

Lack of trust also affects the flow of communication. Experiencing a breakdown of communication in your organization is like trying to communicate with a person who has had total brain damage. Without the brain transmitting information into all the parts of the body, your body cannot function as a cohesive unit. Just like brain damage leads to death, communication breakdown in your organization not only slows you down, but could also kill your organization.

6. No Talent Retention

When there's no trust in the atmosphere, people will walk out. I have found that many will happily take a pay cut and leave an organization they don't trust to be somewhere they feel safe. It's impossible to retain high achievers and great talents in a place like this. When you lose your movers and shakers you lose speed immediately—no acceleration.

7. Destroyed Credibility

One of the most difficult things to rebuild once destroyed is credibility. Once people lose trust in you, your vision, your product, and organization, it's almost impossible to win them back over. When you lose your credibility, sometimes you're better off just starting over with a new brand. No one wants to be associated with people who have a terrible reputation.

8 Things You Must do to Build Trust for Yourself and Your Organization

1. Meet Expectations

Unmet expectations are one of the greatest causes of broken trust. You have to break the habit of overrating yourself. Many people over-promise and under-deliver, which means you need to learn to do the opposite, under-promise and over-deliver. When you over-promise and under-deliver you automatically lose the trust of those around you. You begin to create a track record of unmet expectations and word gets around quickly. This is one area that I used to struggle with. Being a generous guy, my tendency used to be to promise people the world. I would want to solve everybody's problems and fix everything around me. As a result, I would sometimes find myself promising people things out of my kindness that I could not fulfill in my limited capacity—time especially. You can be a great guy, honest, and generous, but if you over-promise and under-deliver, people will always struggle to trust you all the way. This lack of trust slows you down. You also have to be careful of unwritten expectations. Our actions will cause people to expect certain things from us. Be proactive about clarifying and addressing unwritten expectations. This is also a key recipe for a healthy marriage and family.

2. Have Integrity

Integrity is twofold: 1) A person who simply does what they say they are going to do, and 2) a person who lives up to their personal values in the midst of temptations and opportunities to cut corners. Whether people are watching or not, a person of integrity is dedicated to honoring their values. Lack of integrity means that you are compromising your values and continually adjusting them to please those around you. Soon people begin to wonder where you stand on important matters and they question your personal integrity. When this happens you lose people and momentum. But when you walk in integrity you become a people magnet.

3. Cultivate Pure Motives

Many start well with the desire to impact their community and transform lives, but for some it quickly becomes only about success, power, accolades and material things. There is absolutely nothing wrong with success, the right kind of power, and prosperity, but if your primary motive is just about success at the expense of others, you will quickly lose people's trust. It doesn't matter how much you say you are for people, your deepest motives always have a way of coming to the surface. Also because of setbacks and betrayals, some people become motivated by fear, unhealthy competition, and jealousy. Very dangerous. Cultivating pure motives should be a lifetime exercise for all of us. We always have to search our hearts and realign our motives back to the original cause. A person with pure motives attracts people. You become a breath of fresh air. People easily trust you. This is also another key recipe for a healthy marriage and family. Your spouse and children have to know that you look out for their best interests first.

4. Deliver Results

When it's all said and done, you have to have a track record of productivity. At the end of the day that's what it's about: productivity (getting the job done). There's nothing that will drive people away from you and cause them to lose trust in you like giving an excuse for every time you fail to get the job done. You are better off apologizing and making it right the next time. Bottom line: you violate trust when you don't deliver results. Giving excuses communicates that you are comfortable with your failures and that you are not remorse. Most people will give you three chances—three strikes and you're out, never to be trusted again, which means you need to start working on increasing your capacity now. Do whatever it takes to acquire the tools, knowledge, and skills that you need to do an excellent job and meet expectations. You may need to go back to school, get a tutor, a private teacher, coach, whatever it takes to increase your capacity. Of course none of us are perfect. There will be a time when you will drop the ball even on your best day. As long as you have made significant deposits into the trust bank accounts of people, some withdrawals won't damage you. It's the overdraws (depletion) that will kill you.

5. Be Consistent

Consistency communicates that you are dependable and reliable. Being inconsistent communicates the exact opposite. How can anyone depend and rely on you when your results are up and down—always fluctuating like a yoyo? You can be the nicest guy or lady in the world, but as long as you're inconsistent, people will always look at you as someone who's undependable and unreliable—someone they cannot trust or count on 100 percent. You become an inconvenience, and no one likes to be inconvenienced. This will cost you valuable customers, partners, and growth. On the other hand, if you create a track record of consistency, you gain trust, which brings you acceleration.

6. Be Accountable

When you have accountability in place, as a person or as an organization, it says that you are doing the right things and that you are serious about protecting the purity of your vision. Whereas, lack of accountability communicates a false message that you are hiding something. People start to wonder if you have a hidden agenda. They start to wonder if you are involved in something corrupt, immoral or simply not being who you claim to be. This is why you see major growth in companies where they have notable people with impeccable credibility sitting on their Board of Trustees. Ministries, companies, and organizations that have structures that foster and encourage accountability tap into the acceleration found in trust and they grow quickly. Many are suffering in their ministries and organizations today not because they are engaged in something inappropriate or that they lack integrity, but simply because they have not found a way to incorporate the principle of accountability into their structures. Accountability makes people trust you. If you are married your spouse should be your number one accountability partner.

7. Create Functional Systems

Have you ever been at a place where policies are never enforced? Where leaders continually cut corners? Services offered always seem to have glitches? Where there are high levels of redundancy? Where people are extremely bureaucratic and heavily engaged in corporate politics? Turnovers happening all the time? The lack of functional systems communicates that you are either completely incompetent or simply playful (not serious about what you do). Once again, you may be the nicest person in the world, but your lack of functional systems communicates something completely contrary. Eventually, no one takes you seriously and those who are part of your organization become experts at doing the least amount of work. Next, your top notch talent and high achievers jump ship. To keep highly motivated people and high achievers you have to have an atmosphere driven by functional systems. The presence of functional systems communicates that you know what you are doing, you are competent, you respect others, and you are sharp, driven, committed, and dedicated.

8. Extend Trust

When I was about 9 years old my father began trusting me with music ministry opportunities at our church. Then when I was about 14 he began trusting me with opportunities to preach. I will never forget the first time he asked me to preach in a main session at our church's annual camp meeting. This was a big deal. There were about a thousand people there from our other church locations from across the country, as well as guests from all over. Dad himself was scheduled to speak on this big night, and he came to me an hour before and said he felt like God wanted him to give over his session to me. I was overwhelmed with the level of trust he extended to me. Kids that age did not preach on their parent's pulpits or in mega conferences like this. That would be like President Obama asking his teenage daughter Sasha to address the country during the State of the Union Address in his stead. I preached my heart out that night. People were touched, many miracles took place, and the altars were jam-packed. It was absolutely divine. But one thing happened in my heart that night, that encounter changed me for life. Something in me was transformed by the ginormous opportunity that my father entrusted me with. I had no choice but to be a good steward of the trust he extended to me. Making stupid mistakes and embarrassing my father was not an option. From this point onwards, I could not afford to make some girl pregnant or end up in jail like other teenagers were doing. I just could not afford to make a fool of my father and break his heart. He had trusted me with too much and I made a choice that night to not violate that trust. This is what carried me as a teenager. Even when I migrated from Africa to the U.S. at 19, living without my parents in America, I just could not get involved in crazy things because of the trust that had been extended to me. **If you want to build trust, extend trust.** Of course, I'm not saying just trust everyone out there and enable evil people. No. Do the necessary homework and prove character, but afterwards, extend trust.

"The chief lesson I have learned in a long life is that the only way you can make a man trustworthy is to trust him; and the surest way to make him untrustworthy is to distrust him."

-Henry L. Stimson, United States Secretary of War (1940-1945)

5 Key Areas Where Trust has to be Established

1. Personal Trust

First you have to establish trust with yourself. It's impossible to expect others to trust you if you don't trust yourself. Self-trust is derived out of your ability to meet your own personal commitments, therefore increasing confidence in your performance. You have to be a person who's disciplined enough to meet your own commitments first. When you make a commitment with yourself, for example, "I'm going to call my mother tomorrow at 5 p.m.," you need to fulfill that commitment. The more you develop a healthy habit of fulfilling your own commitments, the more you will automatically start to build self-trust. You will begin to gain confidence to trust yourself to fulfill the commitments you make to others. You also increase self-trust (personal trust) by increasing your capacity. As I mentioned previously, acquire more tools, skills, and knowledge in order to get the job done well. You automatically increase self-trust when you have confidence in your ability to get the job done—making yourself worthy of trust from others.

2. Product Trust

After you've established trust on a personal level, the next thing to work on is establishing trust for your product, vision or mission. When people trust you as an individual they become open to your vision, product or whatever it is you have to offer. But that in itself cannot carry you a long way. Their trust in you can attract them to get through the door, but it's the quality of your vision and product/services that will cause them to stay long-term. If it's a restaurant, the food has to be hot, tasty and fresh every time! If it's a ministry or church, the services have to be touching, relevant and well organized! If it's a show, the talent and production have to be stellar. Building trust in your product and services is twofold: 1) Over-prepare. Practice and perfect your craft. Train with a coach—someone who will assess you and push you to raise the bar. 2) Your heart has to be in it and it has to be believable. Make sure your motives are right and that you are doing it for the right reasons. When this foundation is in place you become authentic, genuine, believable and influential—causing people to trust your product. I will expound more on preparation and motives in the chapters to come.

3. Partnership Trust

When people trust you and your product, you build the credibility you need to attract strategic partners and important relationships. Your product, vision, and mission can only go so far without strategic partnerships. Up until a few years ago, Microsoft was the largest supplier of software for Apple. How crazy is that? Aren't they supposed to be the greatest rivals? That could be true, but both Steve Jobs and Bill Gates knew they needed each other. Not only did they need each other, but they also had trust in each other's product. They were both dedicated to excellence and innovating great products. Remember, that while establishing personal and product trust is essential, without establishing trust with strategic partners you will remain limited in your growth and impact. **Personal trust gets people through the doors, product trust makes them stay there, but partnership trust is what grows and expands you beyond limitations.** You have to do whatever it takes to not violate trust with strategic partners. Your trust level, capacity, and ability to deliver have to be high at this level because you work with other competent people at a close proximity. You need to perfect levels 1 and 2 before engaging at this level.

4. Organizational Trust

Organizational trust is on many levels:

- Do team members trust one another?
- Their leaders?
- The vision?
- The systems?
- The structure?
- Do the people trust that the organization cares for their well-being?
- Do team members believe that the services they provide and the style in which they are presented is relevant?

When the right attributes are in alignment, organizational trust is inevitable. It's a proven fact that organizations with high levels of trust function far better and are healthier than those with low trust levels.

5. Public Trust

Now this is the level of greatness. On this level you are no longer just a credible guy or gal with a credible product and great partners. At this level you are on your way to building a BRAND. This is where you build trust as an organization or business with your community, city council, region, nation, or around the world. You start to make a mark on your generation not only because your product is great, but because you are making a great impact on people's lives. I'm not big on soda, but if you look at a company like Coca-Cola, they are a worldwide phenomenon. Brands and companies like Mercedes Benz, BMW, Apple, Microsoft, and McDonald's, have all, over time, established themselves as worldwide brands. Here are the great attributes of these companies and brands that have created public trust at a worldwide level: 1) Great vision and values; 2) great product; 3) growing vision: ability to come up with fresh ideas around the brand, stay relevant and remain on the cutting edge; 4) results oriented: dedicated to a "no excuses" policy where the customer can count on getting what they need; 5) consistency: the confidence customers have that the product is always great; 6) effective: products that not only look good, but solve problems and provide solutions for people; 7) endurance: dedication and commitment to stay in the game. Lastly, I want to say that building public trust also means investing in your community with practical programs that make an impact in people's lives for the better.

7 Benefits of Trust

1. Good physical health

Proverbs 3:8 "Do not be wise in your own eyes; fear the Lord and shun evil. This will bring health to your body and nourishment to your bones."

The fear of the Lord causes you to walk upright and gain the trust of God and men. When you do this, you escape from evil and bring good health to your body. Medical research claims that people who are in a strong and trust-filled relationship are healthier and live longer than those who are not in a trust-filled relationship. Why? It's simply because those people have a strong support system spiritually, mentally, and emotionally. Studies also show that stress is the highest cause of most sickness in America. When there is trust in your relationships at home, in your marriage, and at the workplace, you are healthier physically.

2. Acceleration

Proverbs 4:18 "The path of the righteous is like the morning sun shining ever brighter till the full light of day."

"The path of the righteous..." This scripture is talking about trustworthiness. One of the key elements of righteousness is that it produces a person who is solid and trustworthy. So the scripture says "the righteous are like the morning sun shining brighter till the full light of day"—that's acceleration. It keeps shining brighter and brighter and brighter. There is nothing that will grow your business, organization or ministry faster than when people trust in you, your product and your services. Word of mouth is still the most effective marketing strategy today. Customers will drag their friends and loved ones to you the moment they feel they can trust you and your product. Trust not only gives you growth, but also speed.

3. Credibility

Ecclesiastes 7:1 "A good reputation is more valuable than costly perfume. And the day you die is better than the day you are born."

The value of a good reputation is higher than material things. A good name brings you and your family honor and attracts valuable relationships. You could lose all you have, but if you have a good name, you can get it all back again. This scripture makes one of the most powerful points: a person with a good name is better at their death than at their birth. That simply means that at the time of their death they will be more successful, happier, and fulfilled—acceleration.

4. Valuable partners

Ecclesiastes 4:9-12 "Two are better than one, because they have a good return for their labor: If either of them falls down, one can help the other up. But pity anyone who falls and has no one to help them up. Also, if two lie down together, they will keep warm. But how can one keep warm alone? Though one may be overpowered, two can defend themselves. A cord of three strands is not quickly broken."

There is major value in having a partner. The scripture above says, "Two are better than one." This simply means that the results a partnership gets are better than what each of the partners can attain by themselves. But in order to achieve the grand benefits of partnership, it takes discipline and building a high level of trust. Trust is the glue that holds every partnership together — bringing you acceleration.

5. Marketing

Proverbs 22 "A good name is more desirable than great riches; to be esteemed is better than silver or gold."

When you are trustworthy, reliable, dependable, and kind, you gain a good name. If people can trust you, then you have a good name. And the scripture above says that "a good name is more desirable than great riches and better than silver or gold." Notice how it says "MORE DESIRABLE." It means you could be standing next to a guy who has all the money in the world and people would rather work with you because they trust you. You are more desirable. Also notice how it says "BETTER THAN SILVER OR GOLD." Wow! King Solomon, who wrote the book of Proverbs, was one of the wisest and richest kings who has ever lived. This was the secret to his riches and wealth. He understood that a good name (being trusted by people) was more important than all his riches because he knew that money could run out, but a good name stands the test of time. Solomon esteemed a good name over silver and gold because he knew that if he ever lost the money, a good name is what he would need to make it all back.

6. Healthy culture

3 John 1:2 "Beloved, I pray that you may prosper in all things and be in health, just as your soul prospers."

Healthy culture in an organization, family or ministry is the recipe for acceleration. Healthy culture creates a positive domino effect that produces growth and success. But it takes cultivating trust in order to create an environment that is conducive to creating a healthy culture. I would rather have a small enterprise that has a healthy culture and DNA than have a large one that has a toxic culture. I have dedicated a whole chapter towards this. I will expound on and explain how trust cultivates a healthy culture, and how healthy culture becomes a major benefit—bringing you acceleration.

7. Teamwork

Amos 3:3 "Can two walk together unless they have agreed?"

There is a recognizable link between employee engagement, teamwork, and customer loyalty. Employee engagement is simply the relationship between an organization and its employees. Wikipedia defines an "engaged employee" as "one who is fully absorbed by and enthusiastic about their work and so takes positive action to further the organization's reputation and interests." Companies that engage employees notice a drastic positive difference in customer loyalty and satisfaction. These findings are from a report that was conducted by Best Practices, a business research company. According to data from Development Dimensions International, a talent management consulting company that helps businesses develop systems, a Fortune 100 manufacturing client showed a dramatic 1,000 percent increase in errors among disengaged versus engaged employees. Their findings also state that 75 percent of high-performing companies hold managers accountable for engaging their employees. As a result, when leaders and managers engage their employees and subordinates—cultivating an atmosphere where people trust their leaders and each other—not only do their customers become loyal and satisfied, but high-producing teamwork is established. Trust cultivates teamwork. Teamwork raises the quality of the services and product. Customers then become satisfied and loyal. And then, of course, those customers directly affect the revenues, and bring acceleration and growth.

Key Questions

1. What are the three most important habits you need to break that are standing in the way of people trusting you 100 percent?
2. Who are the three most important people in your life right now who you need to strengthen trust with?
3. Who are the three people in your life that you have broken or weakened trust with that you need to reach out to in order to mend bridges?

Chapter 3

CULTURE

"A toxic culture will eat your vision for lunch any day."
–Dr. Sam Chand

Having a healthy culture in the DNA of your organization, company, ministry or family brings acceleration and success. Many people wonder why they never grow or see significant success even after engaging in all the greatest strategies and cutting edge marketing ideas. They pour out money to develop new products and buy the latest gadgets, but still they find there is no significant growth. The problem is not always with their services or marketing strategies, but most times it's with the culture of the organization. You could have great strategies and a great team of highly competent people, but if the culture of your organization is unhealthy you remain stagnant and frustrated. Most organizations that are struggling to grow are dealing with a "culture" set back. Your organization's culture can work for or against your vision. **Acceleration comes when a great vision is carried by a great team of people functioning in an atmosphere of a healthy culture.**

Defining Culture:

- The daily and weekly habits and routines that govern your organization
- The way of life at a particular place

- How people work together and relate to each other
- The atmosphere of your organization
- The DNA of your organization
- A way of thinking, behaving, or working that exists in a place or organization (Merriam Webster Dictionary)
- The beliefs and customs of a particular society, group, or organization (Merriam Webster Dictionary)

Culture Diagnosis

25 Signs of an Unhealthy Culture (Check List)
1. Lack of honest feedback due to fear of being judged
2. No accountability
3. No defined system for settling disputes
4. Feelings of under appreciation
5. People feel their opinions do not count
6. People feel that their work time is inefficient and ineffective
7. Small vision: no room for high achievers to lead and soar
8. Hurts from the past are harbored and there is no outlet
9. People feel undermined and abused by leadership
10. Underdeveloped people; never upgraded
11. Great insight and knowledge kept to self because of improperly awarded credit
12. Many would not be there if they had an alternative; only there to collect a pay check
13. People are used without relationship; feel like machines (taken advantage of)
14. People have feelings of weariness and being overworked
15. People are more excited about other things they do
16. Poor environment that allows people to compromise values (punctuality, conduct)
17. Majority have issues with the ethics and morals of the organization
18. Perpetual disorder and lack of functional systems
19. Leadership does not do what they say (integrity)
20. People feel they will be cut off/black listed if their personal values differ from the organization's

21. Unclear vision (Where are we going? Where will we be in 3 years?)
22. Unclear expectations
23. Improperly positioned people; not functioning in area of strength
24. Younger generation is not attracted
25. Only one social class is comfortable

- **If you checked 10 or more points on the Unhealthy Culture Check List, you are not in the red, but there is serious improvement needed in your organization's culture.**
- **If you checked more than 15 points, your organization is in an urgent state and you need to get help from other successful leaders to reverse things right away.**
- **If you checked more than 20 points, your organization is in a critical condition. You need to take drastic measures in order to save your organization.**

21 Signs of a Healthy Culture (Check List)

1. People understand that it's not just about getting the job done, but doing it with a right attitude and motive.
2. Team members understand that they are a part of something bigger than themselves.
3. People know that the organization is not made possible by the gifts and talents of a few, but by the sacrifices of many.
4. Team members are willing to sacrifice their own personal interests to promote what makes the team united.
5. Team members understand that those on the forefront are not better than the rest, but they're serving a specific role for the betterment of the team.
6. Team members support those on the forefront just as they would want to be supported if in that position.
7. Treating others as they would like to be treated.
8. People listen with the intent to understand and acknowledge that what is said is important to the speaker.
9. People respond to each other's needs in a timely fashion.

10. People speak calmly and respectfully to each other, without profanity or sarcasm.
11. Team members acknowledge everyone and make every effort to view their perspective.
12. Team members only make agreements and commitments they are intending, willing, and able to keep.
13. People communicate any potentially broken agreements at the first appropriate opportunity with all parties concerned.
14. People look to the system for correction and propose all possible solutions if something is not working.
15. People operate in a responsible manner: "above the line..."
16. People communicate honestly and with purpose.
17. People ask clarifying questions when there's a disagreement or a misunderstanding.
18. Team members never say anything about anyone that they would not say to him or her face to face.
19. Team members continuously strive to maximize internal and external loyalty for the people they serve.
20. Team members make their best effort to understand and appreciate the needs of the people they serve in every type of situation.
21. The team has loads of FUN in the process!

- **If you checked more than 8 points in the Healthy Check List, you are safe!**
- **If you checked more than 12 points, you are healthy!**
- **If you checked more than 15 points, you are simply exceptional!**

5 Foundational Things You Need to Know About Culture

1. Choose or be chosen

Be intentional about developing a healthy culture! Don't lose the opportunity to choose your own culture! Write out your code of values and give them to each member of your team. Otherwise people will begin doing things their own way. Even though it may be out of the goodness of their heart, they will soon create a culture that you may not have wanted. Many get stuck in a place where there are things happening in the organization or your family that are not in line with your values, but nothing is done about it. Habakkuk 2:2 says, "Write down the vision so that those who see it may run with it."

2. Be purposeful

Create your culture to serve a specific purpose. I have found that most of what we call culture is really behaviors, patterns, and habits that were formed by people ahead of us who were in a survival mode. I have heard my Bishop tell a story of a young lady who would always cut off the ends of the pork roast meat every time she was preparing the meal. When her daughter asked her why she did that, she simply said, "That's how Grandmamma did it." They both decided to go and ask Grandmamma why she would cut the ends of the pork roast meat every time she prepared the same meal. Grandmamma's answer was almost comical, "I did it that way simply because my pan was not big enough." She cut the ends of the meat not because she wanted to, but because she was trying to fix a problem—survival mode. Soon that way of cooking became the culture for the family and the rest adopted it. Be purposeful to create a culture that will benefit the next generation.

3. Culture determines your destination

Many people develop great vision, mission statements and invigorating mottos for their organization or ministry. It charges and excites people for a while, but if you are not diligent to imbed your vision into your culture, you end up going in the wrong direction. As a leader you can say your vision and motto is "Team Work," but if you don't have practical strategies, forums, and avenues for people to contribute and collaborate, you will end up in a different destination all together—no team work. People may follow your great vision for a while, but in the long run they will default back to your habits. Many leaders and CEOs get frustrated when their people don't seem to fully comprehend and walk in alignment with their vision. Many invest so much money and hire great consultants to help them communicate vision, only to fall back to the same cycle of old habits and failing systems. Why? It's not because their visions are not great and effective, but it's because it takes a healthy culture to sustain vision.

4. Difficult to change

Culture is one of the most difficult things to alter. Once people have been acculturated to a particular way of doing things, they almost lose themselves if the script is changed on them. This is why once mega corporations decide to bring in a new order they will lay off and remove all those that were trained according to an old culture. It's because it takes more work to change systems, re-educate principles, and alter people's patterns than to just start all over again. While restructuring organizations you can expect backlashes and frustrations to run high. Instead of progressing with acceleration, it actually drags you behind. You need to know this information before you start anything: an organization, business, family, ministry, church, etc. On another note, this should serve as an encouragement to those who have created a great culture.

5. Can be altered with hard work

Well, as much as I have said it is difficult to alter culture, I need to bring a little balance and encouragement to you. If you are in a bad situation with the culture of your organization, it is not the end for you. With a lot of discipline and hard work, if you are determined, you can fix it. I need to be honest that it will require a lot of hard work. It's like trying to teach Americans to become Africans, and Africans to become Indians. It's a total paradigm shift, a total overhaul—complete change. It takes time and patience. If you try to do it too quickly you will damage people and destroy everything. Later on in this chapter I have 7 points that explain how to fix an unhealthy culture and help you regroup.

5 Benefits of Healthy Culture

1. Growth

Like I previously mentioned, healthy culture (one that is filled with habits and routines that execute your vision and code of values) is what sustains the message of your vision. The truth is, failure or success is always traced backed to your daily and weekly habits and routines—your culture. In other words, it would only take me one day at your enterprise, organization or church, to predict whether you will succeed, become stagnant or completely fail. When you are intentional about creating a healthy culture that carries your heart and values, growth is inevitable.

2. Empowerment

In an environment with a healthy culture, people feel empowered. They come alive and are willing to do strategic experiments in their departments in order to break new ground and create new services/products/systems. Also, being in a healthy working environment makes people highly creative and healthy spiritually, emotionally and relationally.

3. Momentum

Momentum is like a stone rolling down a hill. The more it rolls down, the more momentum it gains. Yet, the opposite is also true. If you try to roll that same stone up the hill, momentum works against it. It's like trying to get a bunch of guys to push a truck up a hill. The higher they go, the tougher it becomes. I have found that one of the most difficult things for any leader to do is to maintain momentum. When people are excited about vision, the momentum is high and everyone gets on board. When people are excited about your services and product, the momentum is so high that your whole community becomes walking billboards for you. You spend less on marketing and yet continue to see more people running your way. Again, the opposite is also true. Once people begin feeling agitated and frustrated with your organization or products and services, it's tough to reverse. Healthy culture in your organization is a guarantee to sustain and grow momentum. It's easy to sustain momentum in a place where people feel empowered, motivated and fulfilled.

4. High productivity

When you have a healthy culture where people feel empowered and the momentum is explosive, high productivity follows. All farmers agree that the secret to getting their animals to work for them on the farm is to feed them well and take good care of them. Tired, malnourished and starving cows cannot till the ground for you. The same is true with people. If people are starving emotionally, being abused, underappreciated and overworked because of lack of a healthy culture, they will not produce for you. Healthy culture brings high productivity.

5. Sustainability of vision

One test of a true leader is the ability to sustain what they start. What good is it to start great things and not finish well? You have to ask yourself the questions, "If I suddenly have to leave the company or died today, have I put habits, routines and systems in place that will sustain my vision even in my absence? How long would it all last? Would there be further growth or stagnancy?" If you have not put these things in place then you have not successfully developed the culture of your organization to carry the heart of your vision. It's time for you to start being intentional about developing a healthy culture. Healthy culture gives your vision sustainability.

8 Ways to Create a Healthy Culture

1. Code of values

Habakkuk 2:2 "Then the Lord answered me and said: 'Write the vision and make it plain on tablets, that he may run who reads it.'" You have to write down the code of values for your company, ministry, church, family or organization. Write down everything that matters to you. Don't leave anything out that communicates your heart. Put the list in a place where everyone can see and read it on a daily basis. Along with that, aim to open every meeting or conference call with someone or all the participants reciting the code of values. It's not any good to have your code of values printed in fine print on some random document. They are no good if no one can see or read them. Here is a test you should do: go to 10 of your team members and ask them to recite the code of values. If fewer than 5 people cannot remember them, then you are at risk of creating an unhealthy culture that does not line up to your values.

2. Creating functional systems

This is where the rubber meets the road. Many people have great values that lay dormant because they never created functional systems to purposefully drive their values. After you have effectively communicated your code of values, you need to create systems—activities and opportunities for people to execute the values through. Creating a functional system specifically designed to help people execute your values will take creativity and great dedication. If this is not done, your code of values will be reduced to a mere sign post with no power. Let me elaborate. If one of your core values is to have a work atmosphere where people feel empowered and appreciated, you may want to create a monthly "Day of Appreciation." This can be a day where the entire team will appreciate one of the team members with gifts and words of affirmation. The "Day of Appreciation" becomes a monthly habit and routine, better yet, the tradition of the organization—a tangible vehicle designed to execute your value for empowerment.

3. Accountability

After effectively communicating your code of values and creating functional systems to execute them, the next step is to create a system to hold people accountable. Without accountability, a system to enforce and make sure people are honoring your code of values and functional systems, people will fall off track. That's like asking a bunch of kids to go to school and study for their exams without ever inspecting and making sure they're doing what they're supposed to be doing. **You have to inspect what you expect.** It's human nature to pay more attention to things that you know someone will check up on. Accountability makes us take things seriously. A lack of accountability is one of the greatest mistakes I see. Without accountability systems in place you send out a wrong message that says you don't take your code of values serious enough to enforce them. As a team member you are responsible to do your part and be accountable.

4. Assessment

Here is another critical area. After you have effectively applied accountability systems into the DNA of your organization, you have to take time to review what's working and what's not. People feel a false sense of loyalty to certain policies and systems that they themselves have instituted. It's as if there is an invisible sign that reads, "Once an idea is instituted, never to be removed." So people are stuck doing things that don't work and yet no one can explain or question the reason why something is done. This creates a problem. Egos have to be destroyed and a collaborative forum that can assess and deliberate on what to keep or lose has to be cultivated. This means that you have to cultivate the culture of "Honest Feedback." Create an atmosphere where people can challenge the process with respect in order to find the most effective ways to execute your vision. You have to create an atmosphere where people are not persecuted for speaking their mind. It's a waste of knowledge to have smart people on your team who are simply reduced to manual labor. The greatest asset your team members bring is not manual labor, but knowledge and ideas. Proverbs 15:22 says, "Without counsel, plans go awry, but in the multitude of counselors they are established."

5. Development

Genesis 14:14 "When Abram heard that his relative had been taken captive, he called out the 318 trained men born in his household and went in pursuit as far as Dan." When people are not developed, they don't grow. When people don't grow they become insecure and frustrated. Frustrated people frustrate people—creating an unhealthy culture. As a leader, I have found that very few organizations have a strategic system in place for training their people. I've always found it interesting that leaders will get disappointed or angry with their employees when they fall short on their tasks, yet they don't take the time to train and develop them. **If you don't have a plan for development, you simply have a plan for no growth.** You plan to breed a culture of stagnancy and frustration on your team. You have to be dedicated to adding value to those you serve with. In Genesis 14 we see that Abraham was a leader and had trained soldiers in his camp who were developed for special military missions—keyword "developed." There are four reasons people will follow your leadership: 1) Because of your position; 2) because you have impacted them personally; 3) because you make them better (add value); and 4) because they are captivated by the cause the organization is serving. Those under you can only follow you because of your title and position for a short time. If you don't transition to the other levels, touching them personally, developing them, adding value to them, and having a real cause, they will start dropping off and jumping ship. Lastly, let me say that leaders in actuality help themselves when they develop the people who serve under them. At the end of the day, after being developed, people will perform to the level of their capacity. When you increase the team's capacity, you increase your growth and productivity—acceleration. As a team member, you should also be dedicated to increasing your own capacity and upgrading yourself.

6. Conflict management

Conflicts are inevitable. They will happen. The Bible says offenses must come (Matt. 18:7). You can't avoid them, but you can simply plan how to deal with them when they come. There should be a clear and defined system for settling disputes. This simply means that when two or more people are in conflict, they should know exactly what they are supposed to do in order to resolve the matter. First and foremost, every team member should commit to doing all they can to settle conflicts. "If it is possible, as far as it depends on you, live at peace with everyone" Romans 12:18. When there is no defined method for settling disputes, it is like having giant holes on the bottom of your cup. It oozes and drains the life out of your team. Yet when conflicts are managed well, they become an asset of binding people together and building trust. Trust is not built by superficial relationships that put up a façade—pretending to never be offended. Trust is birthed when people are sincere and honest enough to disagree respectfully and resolve conflicts. A strong marriage is not one that never fights (harboring offenses), but one that fights fair. Here are four levels in solving a conflict: 1) in love, confront the person who has offended you; 2) if it's not resolved, include a friend; 3) if it's still not resolved, bring in a mediator/someone you both would respect as a mentor; 4) if nothing fixes it, call on the conflict resolution board that will bring reconciliation and make a decision that both parties have to respect.

7. Cultivating a winning atmosphere

Matthew 5:9 "Blessed are the peacemakers, for they shall be called sons of God." Everyone on the team has a responsibility to create a winning atmosphere. A winning atmosphere is an atmosphere filled with fun, encouragement, appreciation, unity, collaboration, etc. It's a no gossip zone where people commit to not say anything about another team member that they would not say in that person's presence. People think it's the responsibility of the leader alone to create this kind of atmosphere…they are right, but incomplete. The leader can lay the foundation and become an example, but it will not be done until each member of the team also contributes their great smiles, good attitudes and words of encouragement. As a team member, you have a responsibility to contribute to creating a winning atmosphere. After all, you are the one who has to deal with that atmosphere anyways.

8. Fix yourself

When it's all said and done, the culture of an organization is influenced by the character, habits, and attitude of the leader. You simply produce after yourself. People end up doing what they see you do, not what they hear you say. Your DNA produces after itself. Leaders lead by example. You can't ask your team members to have a great attitude and be nice when you are mean and the first to gossip about your people. If you want a culture of hard-working people, work hard as the leader and remain consistent. Eventually people will work hard and that culture will spread all across your organization. 1 Timothy 4:12 says, "Let no one despise your youth, but be an example to the believers in word, in conduct, in love, in spirit, in faith, and in purity." In this scripture Paul was writing to Timothy, his protégé, and teaching him to be a leader who leads by example. Paul knew that the best way to lead is when you fix yourself and put things in order.

7 Ways to Reverse an Unhealthy Culture

1. Individual conversations

Proverbs 15 "A gentle answer turns away wrath, but a harsh word stirs up anger. The tongue of the wise adorns knowledge, but the mouth of the fool gushes folly." If you are determined to reverse and fix an unhealthy culture, the first step is to go to as many people as possible in the organization and make things right—**take responsibility for where the system has been wrong and paint a new vision.** Your gentleness and wisdom have the power to melt their wrath, let-downs and disappointments. Your wisdom can win them back. This has to be done on a one-on-one level so that you allow people to express how they feel freely. This communicates respect and your willingness to fix things. Be sure to make note of the critical and honest feedback.

2. Cast vision

After successfully selling the vision to the members of the organization on a personal level, call a meeting and share the vision corporately. Be sure to consult with experts and seek counsel from other successful leaders in order to do this well. Invite a few other top leaders to this meeting to help you share the new vision effectively.

3. New systems

Don't just tell the vision and make empty promises, but make some tangible changes and communicate new ways of doing things. Change old systems, habits, and routines and create new ones to prove your seriousness in taking a new direction. This is where people will test you to prove if you are serious about turning things around and building a healthy culture.

4. Feedback

After successfully executing these three points, allow room for honest feedback again. As you start instituting new systems and changing things around, it's going to be a struggle for some people. Open dialog and allow room for people to express themselves. This does not mean that you have to do everything they ask, but it allows you to express and explain to them what's going on—making them feel better and respected. This stage also gives you the opportunity to reassess and see what's working and what's not.

5. Support system

You have to be aware that people respond differently to change. You have to anticipate that some will have extreme struggles with all the changes. Don't wait until people shut down because of frustrations with new systems and routines. You need to proactively put a support system in place to help them cope. Put a system in place where people can be helped spiritually, emotionally, and psychologically. A support system can simply be lending a listening ear to questions through a workplace forum or more in depth through the availability of counselors to those who need help coping with the change.

6. Consistency

When you have applied all of these points, the next thing is to simply remain consistent. Your consistency communicates your dedication and seriousness to seeing change. Your people will be watching you to see that you mean what you say and that you are committed to developing a healthy culture. Even when the going gets tough, remain consistent with integrity.

7. Model change

Again, the culture of the organization is primarily influenced by the leader. If you are serious about reversing momentum and building a healthy culture, you as the leader have to model it. It's going to backfire in your face if you tell people you are committed to fixing things but still behave and do things the old way. The first thing to change has to be you.

Key Questions
1. Is the culture of your organization, ministry or family healthy or toxic?
2. What are the three things you need to do immediately in order to reverse toxic culture?
3. What are the three things you would do differently in the culture of your enterprise if you had a chance to start over?

Chapter 4

SYSTEMS

Poor systems will cripple your vision and place it on crutches. Systems work in conjunction with a great vision to give you acceleration!

S ystems put legs to your vision so that you can move from one position to the next. Dr. Myles Munroe, a renowned expert on leadership, says that the graveyard is the richest place on earth because lying there are not just deceased people, but visions, innovations, books, companies, and ministries that were never realized. The question then is why is it that most visions never see the light of day? Why do many visions start well and then fall off and become extinct? It's because most people have great visions, but no practical or tangible systems to execute them. A vision without systems is like having the fastest runner who is on crutches. Without the full activity of his limbs, a skilled runner cannot win a race. A vision without systems is also like having a Lamborghini without any tires. It really does not matter how much horsepower the Lamborghini has, without the right tires to thrust the car into motion, it's not going anywhere. For the Lamborghini to do its job, there needs to be a collaboration between the horsepower and the tires. In the same way, for your vision to fully be maximized at a speedy level it has to be supported by great systems. **Visions are realized when a great vision is in collaborative operation with great systems.** In this chapter we will dissect this matter of systems, look at various models of systems, and explore precept upon precept on how to create functional systems for the acceleration of your vision.

God never just created things; He created SYSTEMS.

It absolutely fascinates me that in only six days God created everything and has never had to do it again. Just think about that for a minute. God only worked and created in six days. Now fast-forward 4.5 billion years later; we have over 7 billion humans, and more being born every second. We have an immeasurable number of trees and plants, the solar system is still functional; we have billions of animals and fish and water creatures. Yet God did all this in six days and has never had to create again. Why? When you closely observe God's process and strategy for creation, you discover the mystery. God did not just create things; He created systems and empowered them to be self-functioning and self-sustaining.

When you study the book of Genesis, Chapter 1 from verse 11, you will clearly see that God did not create an animal one at a time. He did not create each insect one at a time. God did not create living organisms and plants one at a time. He created cycles and systems: the solar system, human reproduction cycle, plant cycles, animal cycles, etc. He created complete cycles—systems. When God wanted trees and plants, He simply spoke to the earth and empowered it to produce trees. He also made sure those trees would have the ability to produce fruit with seed in it. That seed reproduces more plants and trees. Do you see it? It's a self-functioning cycle. In the same way, when God created man and woman, He put "seed" (sperm) in the man and a womb in the woman. He gave man and woman the ability to reproduce. In order to make brand-new humans, God has never had to come down from heaven again after creating Adam and Eve. He created the human reproduction system. God created systems!

God did not just create the sun, the moon and the stars in the sky; He created the solar system. The complete cycle! God programmed the earth to make a complete 360 degree spin on its axis in 24 hours, which created day and night. He also programmed the moon to go around the earth in 28-31 days, creating a month. Then, He pro-grammed the earth to rotate around the sun on its orbit in 365 days, creating a year. God who exists in a realm of eternity came out of it and created time and seasons by instituting the solar system. As you can observe from this quick study of creation, God's reoccur-ring formula for creation was in establishing systems. These sys-tems were created with such perfection as to function and sustain themselves. God is the source that powers the systems, but the sys-tems themselves function automatically as he programmed them to. Genesis 8:22 says, "While the earth remains, seedtime and harvest, cold and heat, winter and summer, and day and night shall not cease." This scripture implies that seedtime and harvest (the availability of seed and fruit/the cycle) will never cease. Day and night, winter and summer will never cease. God is simply saying that He has set the systems He created to function by themselves until one day when He is ready to shut them all down.

God's Definition of Work

One of the top secrets to achieving maximum success in minimum time is to build systems and processes and put the right people in place to operate them. It's about building systems that are self-sus-taining once you set them in motion. You get more for your time, labor and resources. You simply do a job, set a system in motion, train and empower a team, and get results in perpetuity. That's smart working! Of course, the work of putting systems in place does not happen right away. You also have to be diligent and do some main-tenance work, but putting systems in place allows you to move on to new discoveries and ground-breaking ideas. The systems that you have already set in motion continue producing for you and become a great resource for your new goals. When you have managed to set in motion a self-functioning system operated by great people, you have tapped into what I call "The Speed of Systems." That's ACCELERATION! Those that have discovered the secret of working to build systems versus just working to earn a living accelerate them-selves in a great way. It's God's secret for Acceleration.

God believes in systems! He believes in the art of working to create systems. Too many people are under the misconception that work is a curse. This false ideology is out there mainly because God told Adam, "you shall eat from the sweat of your brow," after Adam sinned against God. So, for many, work is looked at as a punishment. I want to change this way of thinking once and for all. You have to understand that work was mentioned and performed by God Himself before the fall of man. God worked for six days in the beginning and it's recorded in Genesis 1. When Adam sins, it's not until Genesis 3. The kind of work that is introduced after the fall of man is called labor. Before Adam sinned he never had to work for survival. He had everything he needed. He simply worked to fulfill his purpose of taking dominion over all of God's creation and being the master steward. But after He sins he immediately has to work for his survival. There is a difference between labor and God's idea of work. To labor is to provide a service in exchange for money or goods; whereas to work, according to God, is to create self-functioning systems that produce perpetual results. God did it in six days and has never had to do it again because His systems were made perfect. When you labor, you have to do the same job over and over in order to get the same pay. But when you work according to God's model of work, systems, last week's work continues to bring you results and revenue perpetually. Setting systems in motion is God's idea of work. When I talk about systems, I'm talking about internal systems and also strategic models that produce perpetual results. Internal systems are processes within an organization, company or business that are designed with the sole purpose of executing your vision. Whereas models are simply proprietary ideas or processes that have the power to earn you profits in perpetuity.

Think Systems!

Dr. Sam Chand is one of the most successful and sought after leadership consultants today. Who would have thought that Chand, who in 1973 was a student and janitor at Beulah Bible College, would later return in 1989 as president of the same college! Under his leadership, Beulah Bible College became the largest predominately

African American Bible College in the U.S. At the peak of his career, Chand made a critical decision to quit as president of Beulah to concentrate on building his personal leadership consultation company and ministry. At the time, he was taking a major pay cut with this transition, but he knew that eventually this move would earn him a greater return. Today Chand is a millionaire with multiple great selling books, a thriving consultation company, and an impactful leadership training ministry that is raising up a new generation of leaders. While I'm sure a large weekly paycheck from Beulah was comfortable for Dr. Chand, it was simply labor. He would have had to work the rest of his life for that same paycheck. Whereas now he is writing books, developing functional systems and processes for companies, and doing the kind of work that earns him royalties and long-term revenue. Thinking systems simply means thinking about ideas and the kind of work that brings you long-term results. It's thinking about things that create perpetual rewards for you versus one-time rewards. You have to indoctrinate yourself to become someone who thinks systems. I would rather you pay me $200,000 in installments over the next 2 years, than pay me $100,000 today. This is the recipe that multi-billion dollar credit card companies are built on. They are okay with giving you and me $20,000 to buy a car today and in turn get back over $60,000 over a period of 5 years. They think systems and because of that they earn more revenues in the long run.

Now, I want to be clear that I'm not in any way, shape or form despising those that have regular jobs like Dr. Chand had in the beginning. I have an incredible hard-working father who grew up herding goats and cows in the village of Balaka in Malawi, Africa. He worked hard and ended up as a math and science college professor for years before he became a successful full-time pastor and conference speaker. My father is the reason I'm doing what I do. He is my absolute hero. But what I'm saying is that the regular job you have now should simply be the starting point. The labor kind of work should only be the foundation that you leverage from on your way to building systems. You should wake up every morning asking yourself, "What self-functioning systems or processes can I set in motion and contribute to this world?" Personally, I pray about this everyday. I pray and ask God to bless my four kids with witty ideas. I pray and ask God to give me book ideas, proprietary business ideas, original songs, ground-breaking technological ideas, TV ideas, movie scripts, real estate investments, etc. I think and pray for systems constantly. I also pray constantly for God to give me processes and systems that will execute my visions and create a healthy atmosphere for all those who work with me. THINK SYSTEMS! That's where real acceleration is.

6 Examples of Thinking Systems

1. Instead of making demands on relationships today, focus on building pure relationships with people long-term and then they will give you the moon in the future. Many simply lack the patience it takes to build strategic relationships. Don't ever ask for anything before there is a solid friendship.
2. Even with people that you pay to work for you, you will get more than your money's worth from them if you build pure, sincere relationships.
3. True marketing is a lifetime adventure. The money you are spending today to create platforms and opportunities for exposure may not produce a return for you right away, but keep investing and sowing good seed. When the flood gates of blessings open, it will be HUGE!!!
4. Even though you might earn less money working for yourself today, in the long run, if you have a great vision and are committed to working hard, you will earn more money and enjoy the great privileges of being your own boss.
5. Instead of doing all the work by yourself, you will eventually be more productive if you create a manual and train others to work the process for you. Allow others to do the job for you even if they don't do it as great right away. In time they will grow and allow you the luxury of moving on to greater and more profitable responsibilities.
6. Our ministry and organization, United Night of Worship (UNOW), grew exponentially from a 600 people gathering to over 6,000 in about three years. That's a substantial 1,000 percent growth in three years. Soon we had so many people from other states

and countries calling us to come and host a UNOW. I knew that I would strain myself, my team and my young family if we were to go to every state calling on us to raise hundreds-of-thousands-of-dollars and host all of these UNOWs. We decided to think systems. We developed a blueprint and began training others with our model and awarding them with our logo and ministry brand upon their signing of an agreement. Our partners would assume all the responsibilities for their UNOW, including financial responsibilities. It would be an honorable partnership: we were blessing them with knowledge and a credible ministry brand, and they were blessing us with their partnership and the extension and growth of the ministry God gave us. This was not an easy thing to do. At the time, it felt like we were giving up our own vision. It was like handing over our baby to someone else. But the vision had grown beyond us and needed to be released. We were thinking systems! We were thinking long-term! We were thinking influence! We were thinking maximization! After seven years of ministry, UNOW is in 10 states with many more requests from other states and nations outside America. We have grown from gathering 600 people in one state to over 30,000 annually in multiple states and many souls that have been saved, healed and delivered. Our network of pastors and churches is in the thousands. And through our partnership with God TV, we are also able to broadcast to over half-a-billion-people worldwide in over 200 countries. I recognize that God's grace has been abundant. We are so grateful and give all glory to God. I know without His acceleration secret found in systems, we would have limited the vision.

Don't just think about what you desire to earn today; THINK SYSTEMS—long-term!

13 Signs that Indicate Lack of Effective Systems (Models and Internal Systems)

1. There is no blueprint or manual present or visible in your organization or ministry instructing people on how to get specific jobs done.

2. If you stopped working today, none of your projects would continue earning you money or resources.
3. If a department leader left the job suddenly, the new leader would not have a clue on the operations of the previous leader.
4. Lack of uniformity. Every one in the organization or ministry does it in their own way.
5. No one in the department can teach the process with full confidence that they are representing the official process of the organization.
6. People do not seem to know what or how they are expected to get the job done.
7. Because of the lack of timelines attached to systems, people continually miss deadlines and always seem to be flying by the seat of their pants as they strive to manage various projects.
8. There are high levels of frustration especially among the elite workers and high achievers due to lack of real systems.
9. Inconsistent results and frequent turnovers.
10. Lack of measurable results.
11. Senior leaders are stuck and forced to improvise even on what should be entry level responsibilities.
12. Breakdown of communication across departments.
13. There is an extremely bureaucratic atmosphere where people waste more energy trying to prove their methods than doing their work.

5 Examples of Business Models that have Accessed the Speed of Systems

These are just a few examples of the principle of the Speed of Systems:

1. Franchising model

Like McDonald's and many other food chains, this is a system and model where you award qualifying partners the use of your business processes and brand for a fee and royalties. Your partners help grow your brand while sharing some major responsibilities with you, including financial responsibilities. This is why there are over 33,000

McDonald's worldwide today. It's a shared responsibility among thousands of business persons. This system can be applied in many other spheres of life to release acceleration.

2. Real estate

Like Donald Trump, those who buy property and land low and sell high or rent, earn a good profit.

3. Royalties

Royalties can be from books, songs, movies, etc. The Beatles still earn millions of dollars in royalties from songs they wrote and recorded many decades ago.

4. Proprietary ideas

Proprietary is defined as "something that is used, produced, or marketed under exclusive legal right of the inventor or maker" (Merriam-Webster). Examples include: innovations, inventions, computer software and operations, manufacturing processes, etc.

5. Licensing deals

A licensing agreement is a legal contract between two parties, known as the licensor and the licensee. In a typical licensing agreement, the licensor grants the licensee the right to produce and sell goods, apply a brand name or trademark, or use patented technology owned by the licensor (inc.com). Your single idea can earn you a fortune. For example, Bill Gates created Microsoft Office, computer software that facilitates operations for office needs. There's Microsoft Word for writing, Microsoft Excel for data entry, Microsoft PowerPoint for presentations and many other facets. They have a version for individuals and another for businesses, all compatible for both PC and Apple. Microsoft operations are also used in phones and iPads and applied to many other platforms. Every time an individual or a company downloads Microsoft Office they are required to pay a substantial licensing fee. What's fascinating is that Gates created and introduced Microsoft Office back in 1988! Today Microsoft Office is the premier product for office work worldwide, and over 25 years later since its inception, Gates is still making millions annually from Microsoft Office alone. Isn't that just super fascinating? He is making money from work he did over 25 years ago! This is exactly the model that God established when **He created systems in 6 days, over 4.5 billion years ago, which still function today!**

5 Ways Franchising and Proprietary Systems Accelerate You

1. Reproduction factor

A true proprietary idea has power to sustain and reproduce after itself once you have worked hard to set it in motion. This is true when we examine God's systems: humans, animals, plants and trees all reproduce by themselves. Once you get that proprietary idea that others are fighting for, you are guaranteed royalties from just that one idea. While you are at the club playing golf, that idea is working for you. Once you train your team on how to systematically get the job done and empower them to do the job, you can move on to the next task while the previous one is still in motion and producing for you. This is what I call the reproductive power of systems. This reproductive power brings maximum speed in minimum time. You can be earning royalties from a book or song that you wrote 20 years ago. That's reproduction. Without systems you waste your valuable time doing the same thing over and over for the same pay.

2. Less labor management

When you own a restaurant you have a 100 percent responsibility to hire people to do the work of managing and sustaining the company. But when you own and operate a franchise, the responsibility to hire labor to manage and keep the restaurants functional is not on you alone. Your partners (franchisees) who run your restaurants have the responsibility to hire and manage people. Can you imagine if all the 33,000 McDonald's restaurants were owned by one person?

That person would have to hire and manage thousands of employees worldwide. That would be a painful and time-demanding process. With the franchise system there is a shared responsibility for labor management. You work less and accomplish more. You achieve maximum success in minimum time. It's the same with internal systems in your organization. When you teach the process and empower others to lead, do the job, and work the system, those subordinates also take the responsibility to attract and pull in other competent people. You don't have to waste time looking around for gifted people to join your operation. The people you empower become your greatest assets for discovering new talent. This only happens when the leadership is secure enough to empower people and a give them a sense of ownership.

3. Reduced financial pressure

Just as I previously mentioned concerning shared labor management, there is a shared responsibility in the area of finances when you establish systems. Once again if it's in the franchising model, it's the franchisees (your partners) who raise the entire capital for each new restaurant. When you allow people the opportunity to own stake in a business, you also require them to assume financial responsibility. All you provide as the owner is the blueprint consisting of the vision, brand, process and how to work the process. You don't have to come up with all the capital every time there is a new restaurant. You have minimal to spend to maintain the businesses. Your partners (franchisees) carry that load. That is acceleration. As a result, you end up having more impact and making more money even while you are working on or doing something else. It's a great deal. It reduces your financial pressure while growing productivity. The same is true with the real estate business. When you decide to buy a three-family house instead of a single-family, rent from the other apartments covers a considerable portion of your mortgage. As the owner, you end up paying less, and in some cases living mortgage–free. There is a reduction of financial pressure to the owner. It's also the same with internal systems for your organization. When there is an established system for getting the job done, it's easy to project what your needs are. An accurate projection derived out of your systems also allows you to make accurate projections on the resources you will need — acquiring resources inexpensively.

4. Greater partnership

No one wants to spend the rest of their life just building another man's kingdom. People may be willing to do that in the beginning, but there comes a time when that season simply expires. Unless you empower people and give them a sense of ownership, they will grow weary and lack true fulfillment. When you have stake in something you work harder. You are invested in a greater way. This creates a good ground for great partnerships. It's through great partnerships where great innovations are created — where all parties of the partnership are dedicated to bringing their best for the betterment of the company, ministry, or family. The way to get the best out of people is to respect, honor, and trust them with the responsibility to become a partner. This also works internally when you promote competent people to assume responsibility over certain systems within your establishment.

5. Greater focus

When people know the process from A-Z, they buy-in and are focused 100 percent. People want to understand the processes that should be implemented in order to produce great results. People love to be effective and efficient. It's absolutely frustrating working in an environment where the process (system) is broken, non-existent or not clear. It's tedious working in a disorganized environment. People tune out and become highly unmotivated. Yet, when the systems are in place there is greater focus. Focus is a catalyst for high productivity. Companies, ministries and organizations that have functional systems are not only more productive, but also create healthy environments for the people that work in them. When Steve Jobs was just 30 years old, insanely successful, gloriously wealthy and a worldwide phenomenon, it all came crashing down as he was forced out of Apple, a company he had built into a billion-dollar machine.

It was a public humiliation and simply one of the darkest seasons of his life. In 1997, after Apple had failed to deliver, Jobs was re-hired and later on Gil Amelio, the then current CEO of Apple, was let go. Upon his return, Jobs noticed that Apple was producing a random array of computers including a dozen different versions of Macintosh computers. After a few weeks of intense product review sessions, Jobs got fed up. He made an executive decision to only focus on four computer products and cancel the rest. As a result, they were able to perfect their internal systems and lift the company from the verge of bankruptcy. Functional systems produce focus. Focus brings productivity and growth. **Saying no to the unnecessary is just as important as saying yes to the necessary.**

7 Effective Ways to Implement Systems (HOW TO DO IT!)

1. Write the blueprint

Developing a concise and comprehensive blueprint is where it all starts. Take time to develop the manual and make sure you have covered all the necessary areas. Here are a few points that great blueprint/manuals should have:

- Vision: state the vision, mission and purpose of the company, ministry or organization. This is not about writing impressive mottos that don't make sense and have nothing to do with your vision. It's about communicating what you aim to accomplish with simplicity and clarity. People have to get it.
- Code of values: state all the guidelines and expectations that you have for all who become part of your entity. This should include business performance expectations, conduct, attitude and everything else you expect. Don't leave out anything that is important to you. It has to be communicated here and not later.
- Process and timeline: explain the process and systems that govern your vision. Tell the people HOW to get the job done. How to operate the systems and machines. How to collect data. How to deliver results. A good process should also have a timeline attached to communicate your expectation in regards to how long

the process or system should run. For example: you can tell people that you expect them to advertise an event or a product for 9 months before releasing the product or hosting the event. Write as many processes and systems as possible and include a timeline.

- Agreement endorsement: the blueprint should be sealed with a signed agreement/contract from all parties involved to make it official and legal. If the parties entering the partnership are not serious enough to sign it then you should not move forward. They are probably not in agreement, and if that's the case, the future will be problematic and a waste.
- Terms of termination of agreement: it's also important that the blueprint has clear information on what the acceptable procedure is to terminate the agreement. It's wise to add this to the contract portion of the blueprint.

2. Locate a strategic partner

Locating a strategic partner is the determining factor right from the beginning whether you are going to succeed or fail. Determining the right person to train and empower for the purpose of executing your process or systems is key. This is where most people go wrong. Choosing wrong people to execute the right process produces compromised results. Later on in the book, I have a whole chapter dedicated to how to choose the right partners for acceleration, but here is one point.

- Same DNA: Make sure it's someone who is passionate at what you are passionate about. I know I mentioned about a signed agreement/contract as you enter partnership, but that should never be the driving factor. You should have a qualifying system for your potential partners and team members that is based on them being of the same DNA as you. Having the same DNA simply means that you have similar tastes on creativity, work ethic, and similar philosophies. Notice, I said SIMILAR, not EXACT. You want your partners to be unique in order to contribute new ideas, but you still need to be of like-mind.

3. Training

Whether it's someone becoming a franchisee or simply joining the team to facilitate internal systems, they have to be trained. This is where many go wrong in the process. When it comes to developing a new franchise or establishment, you have to mobilize a team and train individually as well as the entire team together. Below are points of what an effective training should have:

- Blueprint: the training is the place where the blueprint is explained in its entirety. (Show the trainee.)
- Review case studies: helps to be specific to what needs to be learned. (Do the work with the trainee.)
- Role play: allow the team members to try out operating the systems by themselves. (Practice.)
- Collect necessary data that allows you to assess your team so you can better and further help them (Observe and record results.)
- Address all the questions trainees and team members have.

4. Launch with the team

Training and simply awarding the potential team or team member with the blueprint/manual is not enough. As the lead team, you have to launch with the new team. As the leader, you don't have to do the work for them, but you can coach and help build their confidence. Here are a few points on what you have to do as a coach:

- Inspire: remind the ones you are training about the great benefits of the cause and the prize of the goal.
- Motivate: use your personal story of courage and sacrifice to motivate and encourage the team.
- Collaborate: assist and help to do the work when they are stuck with a process.
- Become a lifeline: don't release until you are certain that your trainee is ready.
- Set an atmosphere for them to succeed.

5. Trust and release

After all your investment in training, mentoring and launching the team, recognize that the remaining part is simply for them to experience the work for themselves. The quicker you trust and release responsibility and authority, the quicker the team will develop and become self-sufficient. Many leaders are stuck running all the systems and departments themselves because they never trust and release others to do the work for fear that it won't be done well. They stifle their growth and success because they are busy managing petty responsibilities that should be managed by their trainees and team members. Here are a few points you need to know that will help you to release responsibility and authority:

- Remember where you started. You did not start as a 10; you may have been a 5, 4, maybe even a 2... but you grew as you continued working.
- Stagnancy is dangerous. Remember, if you are not moving on to greater things, you are stagnant.
- There are other ways of getting the job done.
- People you invest time in will always remain loyal to you even during transitions.
- Small thinking is detrimental. It stifles and repels highly creative people.

6. Review and assess

This is yet another important step in the process of teaching systems to your team or franchising your vision. This is where the distinction happens between those that become exceptional or simply remain average. This is an intricate step. There are two mistakes that are made at this level that you should avoid:

- The first mistake is when leaders never make an assessment on the process and the delegates/franchisees after they have handed over responsibilities and authority. Many wait until things are falling apart before they assess and make a diagnosis. As a result, delegates are never supported and resolve to their own ways. Trusting and releasing power and responsibility to delegates is a process, not an event. People are different. Some learn quickly and some more slowly. It's not a one size fits all deal. You cannot time it. You have to leave room for people to get it. Your job is to keep reviewing and assessing, then coaching accordingly.

- The second mistake leaders and trainers make is taking back the responsibility and authority after they have given it away because the delegate or team are not performing at the level they are expected. Taking back authority and responsibility after you have given it away violates trust. When you remove trust, you also remove motivation. I personally believe that that kind of action depletes momentum by 90 percent. You kill morale and the motivation for your delegates to keep trying. Allowing your delegate the opportunity to find out what really does and does not work in real life is what makes them grow to the next level. The best you can do at this stage is become the best coach. There is a big difference between a coach and a teacher. A teacher teaches you out of a textbook and from theory (material they have not necessarily tested or lived out). But a coach teaches you from their life experience and walks you through the process without doing the work for you. A teacher is mostly concerned with you passing the test, while a coach is dedicated to you becoming the best you whether you pass the test or not. 1 Cor. 4:15 "After all, though you should have ten thousand teachers (guides to direct you) in Christ, yet you do not have many fathers. For I became your father in Christ Jesus through the glad tidings (the Gospel)."

7. Upgrade stage

Here is another level that separates those companies and organizations that are exceptional to those that are average. You should anticipate a season where there is a need to upgrade systems and processes. As a matter of fact, your signed agreement and blueprint should indicate a time where the systems and process will be re-visited, reviewed and upgraded. By the way, the term upgrade simply means to build on what's already there. Upgrade does not necessarily mean erasing all the present systems and coming up with new ones. Of course, you can do that if there are systems that have become completely unnecessary, but don't change what's working; just upgrade—improve.

3 Reasons We Need to Upgrade Systems

1. Assignments change

Our systems, business models and processes are designed to serve a specific assignment within our purpose. Many times those specific assignments are seasonal. A season could last 3 years or 30 years. Systems that exist without a specific assignment become useless and a waste of resources, time and energy.

2. Remain relevant

Trends and fashions change; people's needs change, and every new generation redefines itself. If your systems don't change with the times, your enterprise or organization will reach its expiration date quickly.

3. Tune up principle

You cannot play a piano for years without tuning it. Every car needs a tune-up. Your systems need a tune-up. As time goes by, some of your systems and machines start to slow down and the people operating the systems become weary. It's essential to tune-up and revitalize the process.

5 Major Internal Systems Every Organization Needs to Have

1. Relationship building systems

Prayer is God's system for communication so that man is able to walk in relationship with Him. Church, marriage, and family are all set systems (platforms) that God established to facilitate human relationships. What tangible internal systems do you have set in place with the purpose to connect your people? People need to connect business-wise, spiritually, socially, and emotionally. Though your annual Christmas party may be a great avenue for people to connect on a social level, it does not satisfy the spiritual or emotional needs. In order for someone to connect on a deep and emotional level, there has to be a one-on-one strategy. It could be a program or forum that allows the people to open up and share deep and personal things. Most large churches or companies struggle here. They reach large numbers of people without ever defining a strategy for connectivity. As a result, there is no maximization of all the great gifts they possess. People gather in great numbers, yet many feel lonely and isolated. You need to strategize and institute tangible vehicles in the weekly routines of your organization, ministry or family that are designed to facilitate relational growth. There will be no agreement if people don't interact. There will be no agreement if people remain strangers. There will be no agreement if relationships are superficial. **There will be no strong agreement without an internal system for building relationships.**

2. Execution systems

God set up a system of execution when he put a seed in humans, plants, trees and animals. He equipped us with the power to reproduce. Strategize and make sure that every department of your organization has functional and effective processes for execution and productivity. Don't build an organization where people just improvise or experiment.

3. Maintenance systems

I personally believe that many organizations and businesses lose about 30 percent of revenue because they are not diligent in taking inventory of all their resources and assets. I have observed that most people are more consumed with the pursuit of the next big project that will earn them great results and a big pay day. In the process there are a lot of unfinished materials, products and projects that cost the company and organization money as they lie dormant. It's like the car dealer who goes bankrupt because he was more consumed with acquiring new and expensive cars than selling the ones on his lot. With each passing day, those unsold cars cost the dealer a lot of money. What good is it if you are taking steps forward but then always taking steps backwards because you don't maximize on what you already have? What good is it to start new projects when the present ones are not effective and are lacking functional systems? Consolidate and create functional systems in order to maximize.

Think and ask yourself the question, "What systems should we put in place in order to sustain what we are producing?" You need systems for collecting data, systems of analysis, and systems for collecting inventory. Having accurate and measurable records of your resources and materials will make you an excellent steward and help you to maximize your profits. This does not happen automatically. You have to include systems of maintenance in the day-to-day operations of your organization, ministry or family.

4. Growth systems

Hillsong Church, a prominent megachurch out of Australia, has grown into a global phenomenon and is impacting millions across the world with their message of love: 100,000 weekly attendees across their multiple campuses around the world, 10 million Facebook fans, 16 million albums sold, songs in 60 languages, 30 million people singing their songs every Sunday, and more. Their message of love through Jesus Christ is resonating around the world and transforming lives. This did not happen as a coincidence. Brain Houston, the founder and senior pastor of Hillsong, had an intentional vision 30 years ago to build a church with an emphasis of passionate worship music. He prioritized and laid out tangible systems for building a stellar music-based church. At Hillsong there are over a thousand musicians, many of whom are acclaimed songwriters, professional and world-class musicians, gifted recording artists, phenomenal music producers, and world-class recording engineers. This amazing team of personnel manages the day–to-day systems for music production. Houston grew up singing in bands and had a real passion for music.

It's the music of Hillsong that has opened up a worldwide platform for the church. Houston was intentional about creating systems to create world-class music. Have you discovered what systems you need to pursue with intentionality in order to achieve growth? Not only has Hillsong grown, but many on their team have had the opportunity to grow with them. With exponential growth like this, people don't have to leave in order to achieve personal growth, both career-wise and financially. Building a world-class music infrastructure was Houston's system for growth and it has worked out!

Jacob worked for Laban, his crooked father-in-law who was continually cheating and ripping him off. Jacob did not become successful until he devised a system for growth that earned him a lot of wealth. The deal was that out of all of Laban's flock, he would keep all the striped animals and his father-in-law would have the spotless and stripe-less animals. Genesis 30 says Jacob placed peeled branches in the watering troughs so that the sheep would be directly in front of the flocks when they came to drink. When the flocks were in heat and came to drink they mated in front of the branches and produced many more spotted and striped flock. The end of the story is that Jacob ended up with more livestock and became extremely prosperous. I'm not interested in arguing or proving whether Jacob's strategy was legitimately scientific or not, but it's clear that this was a system that worked and produced for Jacob. He had a system for growth and it made him so wealthy that he was able to branch out.

5. Transition systems

This is where most people and organizations lose momentum and make life-altering mistakes. Every organization, company, ministry and family needs to accept and face the reality that change is inevitable—transitions have to be anticipated and planned for. Therefore, there has to be systems put in place to make transitions smooth and with less distractions. At some point people will leave or relocate for various personal reasons. Create internal systems that help you transition people well and smoothly, and your name will gain much credibility.

In order to institute systems for transitioning well, you first have to change your perspective about transition. You have to become secure and not think that everybody who transitions and leaves does so because they hate your organization or company. Transitions are simply a sign of growth. Even though many times people transition on bad terms, that's not why transitions originally exist. Transitions should be accepted as part of growth and a sign of life. One day in the future my son Zenzo will become mature and ready to leave our home. As his parents, my wife Michelle and I are aware that this day will come. Although Zenzo is only 6 years old, and we are far off from that event in life, that thought crosses our minds. We don't fight it. We accept it. The first stage is to accept the fact that transitions will come as people grow. Even though certain people may decide to stay and not transition out, accepting it allows you to settle this in your mind and move on to focusing on your work. When acceptance is there, you can now plan, strategize and create systems to help people transition well.

Secondly, even after our son gets married in the future and transitions out of our home and authority, he will still have a relationship with us. At that point we would have to create new systems in our routines. We could choose to say we will all have dinner together every Sunday, and maybe four times a year we could have father-and-son fishing trips. Whatever it is would have to be instituted as a new system. The point I'm trying to make is that there can be relationships that are mutually beneficial on a personal or business level after transition if you accept the process, plan for it, and strategize well. With the right perspective and systems, transitions can be a major asset.

Key Questions
1. What are the three most important internal systems that you have to create in order to accelerate your vision?
2. Who are the potential people with the skills and qualifications to manage and sustain these systems?
3. What proprietary idea do you have that you have not maximized on?

Chapter 5

ORIGINALITY

Focusing on what makes you unique brings you acceleration.

The first thing the police do when they make an arrest is scan the person's fingerprints. Why? It's because nothing identifies someone like their fingerprints. It's a fact that no one past, present, or future, has ever had, or will ever have your set of fingerprints. This proves that you are an original. You are not a duplicate. God made you so unique that there has never been, and there will never be anyone like you. You are one of a kind. When you discover and maximize this truth you become untouchable. You realize that you are in a lane of your own. You are not competing with anyone in this world, but your aim is to be the best you. Being original and focusing on what comes natural and easy to you is the secret to greatness. When you are doing what comes natural for you, you develop high levels of confidence, creativity, focus and authenticity — accelerating yourself in your field of influence. Originality produces acceleration.

God Made You Unique

Jeremiah 1:5
"I knew you before I formed you in your mother's womb. Before you were born I set you apart and appointed you as my prophet to the nations."

Luke 12:7
"And the very hairs on your head are all numbered. So don't be afraid; you are more valuable to God than a whole flock of sparrows."

In these two scriptures God proves to you and me that He knew who we were before we were born and that He made each of us unique. God says to Jeremiah, "I knew you before you were even formed in your mother's womb." This was a time when Jeremiah was fearful and doubting his calling as a prophet to the nations. God affirms him by telling him that he is unique and an original ("I knew you and appointed you before you were even born"). In Luke 12:7, God tells us the shocking truth that he knows you and me so well that he has even numbered the very hairs on our head! Yes, that includes me and my beautiful balding head as well. **You are at your very best when you are yourself**. No one will ever be a better you than you. Acceleration is guaranteed when you capitalize on your uniqueness and originality.

The Power of Authenticity

The most authentic you will ever be is when you are yourself. Authenticity is one of the top assets that you can have working for you in order to achieve success. Authenticity sells. People are attracted to what's real.

4 Ways to Develop Your Originality

1. Pay attention and discover your niche

Take stalk of what comes easy for you. For me it's the ability to see and communicate vision. I noticed at a very young age that it was natural for me to influence my friends. That's leadership. Leadership came natural for me. Even in a time of crisis and confusion, I always seemed to have a vision and strategy for the way out. I was at my best in the midst of chaos and confusion. Have you paid attention to discover what comes easy to you? Write a list down. After that, compare the things you are doing in your life right now to what's on your list. Are you just going through life doing things based on what others around you are doing or simply what life throws at you? Prioritize your unique gifts and talents and success is inevitable. You will only be remembered by the contributions you made in life, not by the things you emulated.

2. Focus on your strengths

When you discover your strengths and niche, spend all your time developing them. Everyone has strengths and weaknesses. Stop wasting time doing things that don't come naturally for you. Though leadership comes naturally for me, I discovered very early in life that I was a terrible manager. Paperwork and all that organizational stuff is not where I flourish. Although I have made great improvements in the organizational area, I know to surround myself with excellent managers. It allows me to focus on my strength and achieve acceleration.

3. Become unapologetically comfortable with being different

Steve Jobs' biography reveals how weird Jobs was growing up. All his friends knew that Jobs had his quirky and weird ways. He was that kid in the nerdy looking spectacles who was obsessed with computers and electrical gadgets. Jobs became successful because he was unapologetically comfortable with being different. Don't allow people to make you despise what makes you different and unique. You will only be remembered by what makes you different.

4. Be in an environment that fuels and inspires your passion/ uniqueness

It's a great thing to have a sense of originality, but please know that if you don't act on those senses you will start to lose your passion. Tiger Woods had to become a golf player after he discovered that it came easily to him. Even though he was excellent at the game, he still had to practice and hang around people who were also passionate about golf. Avoid the presence of those that discourage the development of your uniqueness and originality. Don't undermine the power they have to kill your passion.

4 Reasons Why People Fail to be Original

1. Lack of discipline

I remember how I felt as a young musician, between the ages of 8 to 15, every time I watched the other kids play soccer. They made it look so enticing that I wanted to quit being a musician. Being a professional musician today, imagine if I had decided to play soccer and throw away my piano lessons? Many people fail to remain in their lane of strength, and end up doing something they are not great at, because they are easily enticed by what others are doing. The grass always looks greener on the other side. You have to discipline yourself and remain in your lane no matter how tempting it gets. You will always be average when you are operating in an area that is not your primary strength. You can't be double-minded.

Ray Kroc, owner of McDonald's franchise, revolutionized the American restaurant industry by imposing discipline on the production of great food. Kroc refused to cut corners and required all the franchisees to follow a strict routine. Seventy-two years later they have 33,000 stores worldwide with a net worth in the billions. Your discipline gives your talent longevity.

James 1:6-8 "But let him ask in faith, with no doubting, for he who doubts is like a wave of the sea driven and tossed by the wind. For let not that man suppose that he will receive anything from the Lord; he is a double-minded man, unstable in all his ways."

2. Lack of endurance

Many of us start well but give up after experiencing some setbacks. We give up on what is our original calling and settle for what seems to be working for others in that particular season. Trends and fashions will always change; stick to your strength and your specialty in order to achieve outstanding results. Every field and sphere experiences high and low moments. Whether it's the housing market or the economy, every dimension of life around you will go through a depression period and a growth period. Those who remain in their field and adapt through the tough times always come out on top and learn some valuable lessons in the process. Don't give up on your primary purpose even when times get hard. In due season, you will reap more to compensate for the slow seasons. Of course, I agree that sometimes you may need to pick up something else (in addition to what you are doing) for a short season in order to make ends meet, but if you can still manage to remain in the game, you will come out on top when the tide turns.

Matthew 24:13
"But he who endures to the end shall be saved."

3. Fear of the future

Many people ignore their primary talents and gifts and focus on something else that can provide for them in that moment and season. Once again, there is nothing wrong with doing something else for the purpose of earning a living, but you will only be great at what your primary gifts and strengths are. I knew a gifted mathematician on his way to becoming a great accountant who ended up off his path and working as a nurse. As great of a career nursing is, it was only supposed to be a means of paying his bills at that present time, but it ended up becoming his primary focus. He should have used his nursing resources to finance his accounting career. It's in your primary gifting that you will soar to greater heights.

4. Lack of confidence

Too many people simply despise what they have. Too many think their primary talent is not good enough. You have to remember that champions are not born champions. They are developed. As you develop yourself in your area of strength, your gift and confidence will grow. God used Moses' stick to deliver an entire nation. The children of Israel were in a dilemma. The Red Sea was in front of them and Pharaoh's army was closing in to annihilate them. When Moses obeyed God to smite the water with his stick the sea was split and they crossed on dry land. How much does it cost to buy a stick? Nothing. The stick was insignificant and of zero value, yet God used it to do wonders. If God used Moses' stick, he can use the little stick (talent) in your hand to do wonders too. Jesus took two fish and five loaves of bread, the lunch of a little boy, and used it to feed 5,000 families! When you take your "not enough" and put it in the hands of God, it becomes more than enough.

Zechariah 4:10 "Don't despise the day of small beginnings..."

5 Benefits of Originality

1. Confidence

When you do something that comes easy and natural to you, your confidence level increases exponentially. Confidence gives you the courage you need to get the job done, and get it done quickly. People follow people that possess confidence. Confidence produces believ-ability. Believability attracts people, and people increase produc-tivity—rewarding you with acceleration.

2. Peace of Mind

Stress level is at its lowest when you operate in your area of strength. Of course you will always have a sense of nervousness when you're doing something great, but your mind is more at ease when that some-thing is second nature to you. A mind at ease is more focused and pro-ductive. Too many people blow their opportunities because they were too nervous and stressed out to get the job done. You can regulate this issue by focusing on your strengths.

3. Creativity

Creative juices flow like a stream when you function in an area of your innate talent. When you are unsure and hesitant, your creativity is affected. Michael Jordan tried playing baseball after retiring from basketball. He was far less creative as a baseball player than he was as a basketball player. Why? Basketball came easy for him. He was con-fident on the court. He had a natural talent for basketball over baseball.

4. Marketability

There is a law in economics known as "The Law of Rarity." The Law of Rarity simply states that the demand and value of a commodity appreciates when it's rare. For example, diamonds are rare and each cut is unique; that's why diamonds are expensive. Since you have your own set of fingerprints, you are a rare commodity. Being original places a high demand on your gifts and talents. But when you try to copy someone else, you become a duplicate and your value depreciates. It's ok to get inspired by others and even use their model, but allow the inspiration to ignite the uniqueness in you.

There is nothing more attractive than something real and authentic. No one is attracted to fake things. Everybody loves an original. Authenticity attracts people to you. You become a people magnet when you are authentic. People are inspired and want to be around authentic people. Marketing experts will tell you that authenticity is a big seller. Originality sets you and your product apart, which acts as a built-in marketing tool that attracts people and accelerates you.

5. Longevity

Your passion is at its highest when you are involved in something that truly represents you. Your energy is great when you are doing something that you are passionate about. That energy becomes your most valuable weapon when you are faced with challenges and opposition. Instead of giving up and walking away in a season of trials, your passion builds resistance—giving you longevity.

Key Questions
1. What is the one thing you do that makes you the most authentic?
2. What things are you focusing on in your life right now that you need to lay down because they don't represent your originality?
3. Who are the three people in your life that most encourage and motivate you to focus on what's authentic about you?

Chapter 6

TIMING

Timing: The instinct and ability to respond to and maximize a great opportunity after having prepared well. Success happens when excellent preparation meets with great opportunity.

Psalm 75:6-7 "For exaltation comes neither from the east nor from the west nor from the south. But God is the Judge: He puts down one, and exalts another."

The real great opportunities are simply providential, but you have the responsibility to be the most prepared you can be for when that kind of opportunity comes your way. There is great acceleration in the place where great preparation meets opportunity. One day of favor is enough to change the whole course of your life and propel you towards greatness.

Timing is Like Surfing

People who go surfing know they can never create a wave, but they can simply train to jump on the waves.

When they want to move fast, even though they know how to swim, they realize that they will move much faster riding on a wave. Some of the best surfers can go up to 24 miles/hour or more! Let's just say that's way faster than Michael Phelps, the fastest swimmer in the world.

The key is the training and preparation to jump on the waves and when the major wave (the opportunity) comes, they go for the fastest ride of their lives.

Even though it's true that you can master the art of creating your own opportunities, and you should, the MEGA ONES come providentially (some call it luck). You can't predict or manufacture the mega opportunities. They come when they come.

All you can do is train and be prepared, so that when the opportunity presents itself you are ready to maximize it. That's why you have to train and be prepared in and out of season.

2 Timothy 4:2 "Preach the Word! Be ready in season and out of season. Convince, rebuke, exhort, with all long-suffering and teaching."

4 Examples of Maximizing Opportunity:

1. Netflix

Everybody knows that Blockbuster used to be the premiere movie rental company in America with over 9,000 stores and 60,000 employees. With the growth of the technology age, it was clear that people were transitioning from renting movies at a store to a more convenient digital method. Our culture was changing as everybody resolved to doing things on their computers and mobile devices. Blockbuster made a huge mistake by not transitioning with the boom in technology and the new trend in culture, which led to their demise. By 2007, Netflix took over and established a new model for renting movies. Netflix's timing was perfect. Since Netflix was originally launched in 1999, they had had room and time to prepare and perfect their product and system. Their preparation was met with an opportunity and they maximized the moment and redefined culture.

Today Netflix has over 40 million subscribers and their revenues are in the billions.

2. iTunes

Just like Netflix, iTunes redefined the music distribution industry. Apple Company, who owns iTunes, is a major contributor to the growth of the technology age. Steve Jobs and Apple understood the needs of the culture and provided a solution for accessing and buying music in a much more convenient way. As a result, music stores worldwide have closed and iTunes has become the new way of life. Their excellent preparation converged with the cultural demand (opportunity) to access music quickly and conveniently—timing.

3. Chipotle

Many people don't know that McDonald's is the highest investor in Chipotle Mexican Grill restaurant. Chipotle, whose motto is "Food with Integrity," is the number one fast-food restaurant dedicated to organic ingredients including organic farm raised meat. It was founded by Steve Ells with an $85,000 loan from his father after graduating from the Culinary Institute of America. Ells and his father calculated that his first restaurant needed to sell over 107 burritos per day in order to be profitable. In just one month they were selling over 1,000 burritos per day, and so they opened a second location, and then more locations. McDonald's was paying attention and noticed the emergence and potential of Chipotle. As a leading worldwide fast-food company, McDonald's was aware that more and more of our world was transitioning into a health-conscious culture. McDonald's wanted a piece of this new healthy culture and they invested quickly. Their timing was perfect.

4. Obama captures Osama

When President Obama got wind that Osama bin Laden was hiding with his family in Pakistan, he decided to ignore the diplomatic procedure to notify the Pakistani government and attack swiftly. Obama had watched how President Bush pursued Osama and noticed that it was the Pakistani government which would always hide and shield Osama. Together with the U.S. Army Commander General, they devised a secret mission and killed Osama and his family. Obama found an opportunity and seized the moment. He married great preparation with a maximized opportunity. Under the leadership of President Bush, the years of pursuit for Osama became a great wealth of preparation for President Obama. He was able to devise an effective strategy because of all the knowledge that had been gathered over the course of 12 years following the devastating attack on 9-11.

5 Things to Know in Order to Prepare Effectively

1. Be faithful with the little

David was faithful with his father's flock in the wilderness. He killed lions and bears with his bare hands to protect the sheep. He was disciplined and responsible. This was the best training, both physically and mentally, that David needed to prepare for his fight with Goliath. Sometimes we don't even know what we're preparing for. He prepared in secret for a public showdown and was elevated. Luke 16:10 says, "Whoever can be trusted with very little can also be trusted with much, and whoever is dishonest with very little will also be dishonest with much."

2. There is nothing like over-preparing

You can never prepare enough. Every day Michael Phelps swims laps that are equal to 8 miles as part of his training (approximately 50 miles per week). No wonder he is one of the most successful athletes of all time with 22 medals by the age of 27. Preparation sharpens your talent. When you invest a lot of time in your preparation, you also develop mental stamina (willpower). This is what drove Muhammad Ali to defeat people who were stronger than him physically and catapulted him as a world champion in boxing.

Steven Spielberg is arguably the best movie director in the world. When he was preparing Jamie Foxx to play the role of Ray Charles, it is said that he made Foxx wear a blind fold for hours every day. He wanted Foxx to go beyond acting and feel what Charles felt being blind. He wanted Foxx to act from his heart, not just his head. You become a genius when you master something so much that it becomes dialed into your subconscious. That's how you sharpen your instincts and begin to respond to opportunities by the speed of light.

As you gain experience and master your field, your instincts increase automatically. You begin to transfer knowledge from your head into your heart and subconscious—increasing your reflexes and ability to do the right thing under pressure.

3. Prepare with a mentor

It's not just about investing hours of preparing, but it's the quality of your preparation that determines success. In order to achieve great preparation, you have to prepare with someone who has already gone ahead of you and is packed with a wealth of experience—someone who has already discovered what works and what does not; someone who is an authority in this particular field. **Practice does not make perfect, it makes permanent.** If you practice the wrong way, you create bad habits. Those bad habits will limit your success. You need someone to show you, not just the right way, but the best way.

4. Understand the culture of the field you are preparing for

Study the protocol and etiquette expected for what you are preparing for. Make sure you understand the rules of engagement. As a worship leader I can't sing the same songs that appeal to people in America when I travel home to Malawi. There are some songs that I do that are great, but they just cannot work in Malawi. And vice versa—certain songs that are big in Malawi would have a huge language barrier here in America. When you prepare, do your homework and study culture.

5. Prepare your character

I will discuss a little more on this point because this is where many people fail. Your character is the foundation upon which your gifts and talents stand on. Some people spend their entire lives preparing their gift (charisma) and little or no time preparing their character. Character gives protection and security to your charisma. If your gifts and talents grow beyond what your character can support, you will collapse. This is how Allen Iverson rose to being one of the most paid athletes in America to becoming bankrupt. This is why Michael Vic rose to being arguably the best quarter back in America's football to losing it all because of his addiction to gambling and running an illegal dog fighting ring. Thank God he has now turned his life around and is using his story to educate the youth. Your success will be short lived if you ignore the development of your character. Reputation is who you are in public, but character is who you are when no one is watching.

5 Ways to Build Character

1. Place yourself under a mentor

Submit yourself under the mentorship of an elder, a seasoned person, and submit to what they say—someone who will tell you the truth even when it hurts. Proverbs 13:20 says, "He who walks with wise men will be wise, but the companion of fools will be destroyed."

2. Make sure you have accountability partners

You have to have a few trusted people in your life that you've freely released to hold you accountable to a higher standard. Many people fall in sin simply because they had no one in their life to keep them in check.

3. Surround yourself with wise friends

Do not be misled. 1 Corinthians 15:33 says, "Bad company corrupts good character." Your friends have power to influence your character.

4. Learn from the tests of life

Character is the way you treat the powerless and the voiceless. It's what you do when no one is looking. Character is the real you when you are by yourself. Character is passing the tests of life by doing what is right in private, including honesty at all times.

5. The process of fire

The process to greatness is just as important as greatness. The process equips you with the character, wisdom, and fortitude that you need for longevity. The pain of process equips you. The pain of process gives you wisdom and endurance. It also makes you cherish and appreciate greatness. The fires of life build character—refining you and preparing the character of kings and queens in you that you will need to operate in high places.

5 Laws of Courage

1. Courage does not indicate the absence of fear

Nelson Mandela once said, "I learned that courage was not the absence of fear, but the triumph over it. The brave man is not he who does not feel afraid, but he who conquers that fear." People think that courageous individuals like the late Mandela were born without fear. It's not true. Courage is simply the resolve to push through the fear and do the right thing.

2. No one is born courageous

There is a myth that some people are born courageous and that some were born with more courage than others. The truth is courage can be developed, but no one is born courageous. There are some personalities that may appear more courageous than others, but at one time or another everyone feels overwhelmed with fear. The courageous ones simply learn how to move on in the presence of fear.

3. Desperation ignites courage

On Jan. 2, 2007, Wesley Autrey was waiting for a train at the 137th Street-City College subway station in Manhattan with his two young daughters. A 20-year-old film student, Cameron Hollopeter, suffered a seizure and fell onto the train tracks. Autrey responded bravely and courageously and saved Hollopeter from being struck by a New York City subway train. This is what Autrey said to The *New York Times,* "I don't feel like I did something spectacular; I just saw someone who needed help. I did what I felt was right." Autrey became courageous and brave in a moment of desperation. Courage is ignited by desperation. Desperation does not only come at a time of great tribulation or danger, it also comes when you stir within yourself a great desire to accomplish something—igniting courage inside of you.

4. Courage requires action

Courage is not courage without action. You have to do something. In the brave story of Wesley Autrey, we see that his courage was sealed by his act of bravery—jumping onto the train tracks and saving Cameron. Courage increases and is developed the more you act out and respond to the moment.

5. Courage is contagious

If you want to be courageous, hang around courageous people. Courage is learned like a good character trait. Thabo Mbeki, who was one the youngest members of the African National Congress during Apartheid, esteemed Mandela and took heed to his advice to flee South Africa for his own safety. In the midst of chaos, segregation, killings and a torn country, Mandela told Mbeki that they would enter into freedom and Mbeki would one day be a leader. Mandela's courage was contagious. Mbeki became very outspoken and was on the forefront in ending Apartheid in South Africa. After Mandela's tenure as president ended, Mbeki became the president of South Africa.

It takes courage to seize the moment and take an opportunity when it presents itself. This is where a quantum leap type of ACCELERATION happens.

5 Things about Opportunity You have to Know

1. God has a fair share of opportunities for everyone

You have to know and believe that God does not play favorites. Human beings can play the favoritism game, but we have to remember that God is not human. Of course, God awards favor and greater benefits to those who walk in obedience because they can be trusted, but He shows love to all. Expect great opportunities to come your way.

2. One day of opportunity is worth more than a thousand days of labor

You may be in a place where your life feels stagnant, stuck, and simply not going anywhere. You may feel that you have not had a moment of great opportunity in a long, long time. I want to encourage you and remind you that one day of opportunity can erase the pain you are feeling and recompense you. It takes just one day of favor and great opportunity to restore all you've lost.

3. Sometimes your eyes have to be opened to the opportunities around you

I was in a situation where I needed a music director for our ministry, United Night of Worship, to meet the demand of our large meetings. After interviewing and exhausting a list of prospects, it dawned on me to look within. A pre-existing member of our band not only became a great music director for our team, but also became one of our valuable leaders in our organization today. Sometimes we have everything we need around us, but our eyes have to be opened to it.

4. Sometimes you have to take your opportunities

Our ministry grew exponentially and rapidly. Our first meeting in 2007, had about 600 people and in 3 years, in 2010, we saw over 6,000 people at Agganis Arena at Boston University. That was over a thousand percent growth in just 3 years. Prior to going into the Arena, in 2009, we had gathered at MIT where about 2,000 people packed the auditorium. We had to close the doors and sadly approximately 1,000 people were stuck outside due to limited space. We desperately needed the Agganis Arena in order to grow, but they were just giving us a hard time. I refused to quit and give up. At one point, I would visit the Arena offices weekly — many times without an appointment and unannounced. One day I showed up with our ministry's COO, a tough Irish man named Dan McCarthy. Dan, who has an impeccable resume as a financial manager, was in their face demanding that they give us the arena — and they did. Sometimes you have to take your opportunities.

5. There is always another opportunity coming

As long as you are alive and breathing, that's guarantee that another opportunity is on the way. It may not be an opportunity in the size that you are expecting, but you also have to know that opportunities come in stages. One stage of maximized opportunity propels you and prepares you for the next stage of opportunity. Don't despise any level of opportunity. Your job is to simply prepare well and maximize the moment.

Key Questions
1. What are the top three things I should do every day to prepare for my destiny?
2. What are the top three things I must do every day to perfect my gift(s)?
3. What are the three opportunities in my life right now that I need to maximize?

Chapter 7

MENTORSHIP

My father is one of my greatest mentors. He has been a pastor and preacher for over thirty years. He came from being a scientist and a college professor to becoming a successful preacher and founder of the church he has been leading for the past 30 years. Since my grandfather was not a minister, and died before my dad was 10, my father did not have the advantage to learn pastoring from him. Dad did what most people do, he learned ministry through the tough method of trial and error. Thankfully for me, when I went into ministry, I had my father to learn from. He mentored me and imparted into me 30 years of knowledge and experience. Do you know what this did for me? It accelerated me 30 years ahead. He gave me the wisdom that took him 30 years to accumulate in a short period of time. He put me at an advantage 30 years ahead. I came into ministry with greater confidence and a wealth of knowledge because of his mentorship.

A mentor accelerates you by giving you the knowledge, skills, and experience to advance you past years of trial and error. You discover what works and what does not without suffering through the frustrations of trial and error. Of course, there are going to be areas where you've been given a measure by God to break into new ground-discovering things. Reserve the experimentation for those areas, and allow yourself to learn the majority of what you need to know from someone who has already traveled that path.

7 Ways a Mentor Accelerates You

1. Gives you their time-tested and proven strategies and recipes.
2. Helps you maximize your time by saving you from wasteful experimentation on failed strategies.
3. Helps you maximize your resources and money to invest in what works.
4. Holds you accountable and keeps you focused.
5. Allows you to learn from his or her mistakes to save you from making the same unnecessary and costly mistakes.
6. Keeps you humble by correcting you when you are wrong and protecting you from the dangers of pride and over-confidence.
7. Coaches and guides you for maximum success. In the biography of every successful athlete, there is a name of an exceptional coach. Without mentioning Phil Jackson, you have not adequately told the story of Michael Jordan.

7 Ways to Cultivate a Healthy and Productive Relationship with Your Mentor

1. Pursue your mentor

Many people sit down depressed waiting for someone to reach out to them and offer to become their mentor. Even though a good mentor will reach out to you from time to time, you cannot wait around and expect your mentor to pursue you. Elisha pursued Elijah even though Elijah would always leave him behind. You are the one who needs the help; humble yourself and pursue your mentor.

2. Shut up and listen

What good would it be for you to spend the whole day with Donald Trump and you do all the talking? You are the one who needs to learn about finances, not him. Ask important questions and then zip your mouth and listen. Talk when your mentor asks you a question.

3. Write it down

Take a paper and pen when you have the opportunity to sit at your mentor's feet. You don't want to ever forget the priceless lessons from your mentor. This also makes your mentor take you seriously.

4. Prepare before an appointment with your mentor

Have a notepad with well thought out, life-changing questions. Ask yourself, "What do I want to get out of this mentoring session?" Your mentor will honor you when they realize that you value their time.

5. Be honest with your mentor so you can receive accurate help

You can impress your friends, but your mentor should be the last person you are trying to impress. You will only be helped at the level that you are willing to be honest.

6. Trust them

Find a mentor with a track record of the success you are looking for and trust them. Without the trust factor, you limit yourself to how much you can glean from your mentor. Find the right person, trust them, and then follow through the process.

7. Set a schedule with your mentor

Whether it's three times a year, once every month, or two phone calls per year, without a schedule you will not be productive. Your mentor will take you seriously when you make a demand on them and create a solid schedule. You will not always relate to your mentor 100 percent. Stay the course and learn the knowledge you need.

7 Examples of Great Mentors

1. Phil Jackson

Michael Jordan was a gifted rookie when he started playing for Coach Phil Jackson in the Chicago Bulls. Many agree that if it wasn't for Coach Jackson's guidance, even though Michael had extreme innate talent, he would not have become one of the best basketball players of all time.

2. Joe Jackson

Many believe that Michael Jackson was the best entertainer of all time. What most people don't know is that Michael was raised under the leadership of a tough disciplinarian, his father Joe Jackson. Mr. Jackson made Michael practice daily for long hours—building the work ethic of a genius.

3. Richard Williams

The Williams sisters have won many world championships in the game of tennis. It's because their father, Richard Williams, helped them discover their passion for tennis at a very tender age and guided them through all the stages of their careers.

4. Earl Woods

Tiger Woods has won many world tournaments in the game of golf. At his father's funeral he gave a moving speech attributing his gift and achievements to his father's mentorship.

5. Jethro

Moses became a leader over millions of Israelites overnight. He made a lot of mistakes trying to do everything by himself until he was on the verge of a nervous breakdown. His father-in-law, Jethro, mentored him and gave him a functional system of delegation. This saved his life!

6. Elijah

Elijah had tendencies of a harsh mentor. He would continually leave Elisha behind. He was unpredictable and he kept his protégé Elisha on his toes. But when it's all said and done, he trained and equipped Elisha well and left him with a double portion of his power. It is recorded in the Bible that Elisha performed twice the number of miracles than Elijah.

7. Joseph

Joseph was Jesus' father on earth. We know that Jesus was born of the spirit to a virgin teenager named Mary. Mary was engaged to Joseph at the time and an angel appeared to Joseph to confirm of the coming of Jesus. Joseph spent time with young Jesus, teaching him life's lessons through the skill of carpentry.

There is No Limit to the Number of Mentors You Can Have

Proverbs 15:22 "Without counsel purposes are disappointed: but in the multitude of counselors they are established."

Most of the people who dare to have a mentor limit themselves to just one; and most don't even spend enough time with that one mentor. The scripture above says that in the multitude of counselors (mentors) purposes are established. "Counselors" is plural. This implies that it's not just about having one mentor, but having many of them. You need mentors in all the key areas of your life in order to have good success. Sometimes you may have a mentor who is knowledgeable in several dimensions and spheres of life. I have a mentor who is knowledgeable in the areas of ministry, finance, marriage, parenting, and health. So I'm able to touch all the 5 key areas of my life from this one person who I cherish greatly.

5 Key Areas Needing Mentorship

1. Spiritual

Your relationship with God your Creator is the most important area. Without this it's impossible for you to fully discover your purpose in life. God is your source. You cannot watch your TV without first plugging it into the power source. That's how you get power. God is the source of life. Without being plugged into God, it does not matter how alive you think you are, you are spiritually dead. You need to plug yourself in every day. You need to value your time of devotion, which is simply separated time talking to God and learning more about who He is. You also need to maintain a relationship with a spiritual mentor—someone who is ahead of you in their walk with God so that they can teach and guide you in the ways of God. It could be your pastor, parents or rabbi. Samuel was born to be a great prophet to the nation of Israel, but it took Eli the priest to teach him how to hear God's voice (1 Samuel 3).

2. Health

After God, you and your health are the next most important thing to your life's priority list. You need to have a mentor in this area. You cannot be good and beneficial to your family, friends and community when your health is deteriorating. Find mentorship: personal doctor, nutritionist, personal trainer, etc. Be consistent in your relationship with them. Schedule meetings and set a routine where you can sit and spend time with your mentor consistently.

3. Family

After you, your spouse is the most important person in your life. For those who are not married, it's your family (first your parents, then siblings). For the married people, your spouse should be your priority over your kids. After all, your kids are at their best when they are being raised in a healthy and loving home. Isn't it interesting that we go to school for a long time to study for our careers and yet we despise having marriage counselors to teach us how to have a healthy marriage? Make it a priority to get a mentor for your marriage: professional counselors, pastors, elderly couple, attending a marriage seminar/conference once a year to refill your marriage tank.

Parenting

This is an area no one can afford to make mistakes. Find a couple that has done exceptionally well to raise their kids and seek them out for advice and mentorship. Don't ignore your kids because you're chasing a career. Your kids should be priority over your career. I know the number one argument most people with demanding careers have is that they are trying to become successful so they can better their families. The problem is most people become successful at the expense of their kids. Of course, money helps you to do more for your family, but what your kids need most is you. Quality time with your kids fills their emotional tanks.

4. Career/Ministry

Many people dread going to work because they feel stuck doing something they are not really passionate about. Many people have degrees in practices they are not passionate about. Your passion or conviction in life helps you discover your purpose (the thing you were born to accomplish). Out of your purpose a vision is born (a vision is a platform that helps you to live out your purpose). When your career is in line with your passion, conviction, purpose and vision, you attain good success. There's a difference between mere success and good success. Good success is the kind of success that comes with no sorrows or heartache—fulfillment. You need the help of a good mentor to discover your purpose and passion in life. A good mentor will help you achieve good success.

5. Financial

This is an area where many of us make astronomical mistakes. There is such a stigma around financial matters that many people don't like to ask for help. It's as if there is an invisible rule that says you are just expected to know how to manage your finances all by yourself. Find someone who has been successful in managing and growing their finances and allow them to walk you through the process one day at a time. The way you handle your finances reveals your true character.

Key Questions
1. Do I have mentors in the 5 key areas of my life?
2. Who am I going to approach to mentor me?
3. How many times will I meet with my mentor every month/year?

Chapter 8

PARTNERSHIP

Ecclesiastes 4:9-10
"Two are better than one; because they have
a good reward for their labor.
For if they fall, the one will lift up his fellow: but woe to him that
is alone when he falleth; for he hath not another to help him up."

The Bible also says that one will put 1,000 to flight, but two people together will put 10,000 to flight. Wow! From a 1,000 level to a 10,000 level simply by getting a partner; that's a 1,000 percent growth. Anyone in business will tell you that a 1,000 percent growth is extremely substantial. There is a 1,000 percent increase in growth as soon as you join efforts and partner with someone else who is skilled and wise. How would you like to get an instant 1,000 percent growth in whatever it is that you are doing? I love how the scripture puts it, "Two are better than one for they have a good reward for their labor." A good reward in this case is implying that they get more results for what they both individually put in. They get more and get it faster! That's acceleration!

God has endued success in the principle of partnership and agreement. In Matthew 18:19 Jesus makes a promise and guarantees it. "Again, truly I tell you that if two of you on earth agree about anything they ask for, it will be done for them by my Father in heaven."

Jesus does not say "it might" be done by my father in heaven. He says "it will." Partnership accelerates you!

5 Benefits of Having a Partner

1. You increase your assets

We all have assets and liabilities. Your talents, finances, resources and skills (anything that works positively for you) are your assets. When you partner with someone else with a set of assets that compliment yours, you increase your assets immediately and build an irresistible team. That's one of the success secrets of Apple. Steve Jobs and Steve Wozniak brought their assets together to form the foundation of one of the best companies of all time, Apple. They brought their assets and capital together; Jobs was the marketing and branding genius while Wozniak was the engineering/technical genius. No surprise they rose to the top.

2. You minimize your liabilities

Ecclesiastes 4:10 says, "For if they fall, the one will lift up his fellow: but woe to him that is alone when he falleth; for he hath not another to help him up." Loneliness, fear, doubt, failure, debt, areas of ignorance, and lack of needed skills are all liabilities. When you have a partner you are able to receive encouragement, emotional support, and financial backup. You get the benefit of the skills you don't have and you get them for free. A huge challenge becomes lighter when the burden is shared between two or more people. Instead of being crushed and destroyed by a challenge, you are able to survive and regroup when you have someone else to endure the problem with.

3. Greater strategies

Growth is all about executing strategies and ideas that work. Show me your strategies and I can predict where you are going to be 20 years from today. When two minds of similar capacity come together to brainstorm and dream, greater ideas and strategies are birthed. You become better than what you could have become on your own.

4. Shared responsibilities

Is it easier to lift and move a couch by yourself or with the help of another person? Of course it's easier with another person. With two people you are able to balance the couch, share the load, and move it easily. It's not always a matter of managing the weight, but also the simple fact that the shape of the couch requires two people in order to balance. That's what you get with partnership. You share the work load and, most importantly, you achieve a healthy balance in what you do.

5. Fast production

When I was little growing up in Africa, my mother would take us to the farm during harvesting period to help with harvesting corn. After bringing home hundreds of bags filled with corn on the cob, the next duty was to peel the corn off the cobs, bag it up, and send it off to the mill machines where they would produce flour out of it. The only way to peel the corn from all the cobs and get the job done fast was to get more people involved. The more hands we had, the faster the job got done. Partnership gave us speed.

7 Qualifications to Look for when Choosing a Partner

1. Someone with the same values as you

Be sure to pick someone who values people, is respectful, faithful, reliable, dependable and polite. Your partner's good or bad reputation reflects and affects you. Your vision is influenced by the set of values that are important to you. If you pick a partner with a set of values that conflict with your nonnegotiable values, you will have division. Two words: Di-Vision. "Di" means two. You will have two visions—lacking the laser kind of focus that produces success.

2. Someone whose set of skills and talents compliment yours

I loved the partnership between the heavy weight boxing champion Muhammad Ali and his coach Angelo Dundee. These two were an unstoppable force. They were a great partnership because their set of skills complemented each other. Ali fought and Dundee trained and managed Ali's career. Dundee understood Ali's fighting skills, but also his intricate personality. Ali did the fighting, but also trusted the wisdom and counsel of Dundee. Because of this partnership, Ali arguably became the best boxer of all time. Each one was content doing their part and they both did it well. Even though there will be times when your set of talent and your partner's may overlap, finding someone who has a set of skills that compliment yours is crucial. You don't just need a duplicate of yourself in your partner, but someone whose set of skills and knowledge puts you at an advantage.

3. Someone with the same measure of passion

You can never convince someone to be excited by what excites you. You don't want to waste valuable time motivating and trying to get the buy-in of someone who is supposed to be your partner. You can't accomplish anything with someone who lacks vision and is unmotivated. Michael Jordan and Scotty Pippen were both passionate about basketball and becoming champions. They broke records in the game of basketball together because they had the same measure of passion.

4. Someone who pulls their own weight

The last thing you want to do is babysit someone who is supposed to be helping you. You could easily waste valuable time and miss your moment dealing with someone like this for a partner. Trying to carry a heavy marble piece of furniture with someone who is not pulling their weight is not only a path to failure, but it's dangerous. It's dangerous to partner with someone who is lazy, scatterbrained, unfocused and quick to give excuses. If you are in business, at the end of the day all your clients care about is if the job got done, not listening to excuses. Get someone responsible, tenacious, enthusiastic and productive. One of the major advantages to having a partner should be that you are able to take turns running your enterprise if need be. You should be able to take care of something else or take turns going on break with full confidence that your partner is capable of running things on their own.

5. Someone who is wise

Not everyone who has knowledge is wise. Wisdom is the ability to apply knowledge instinctively in real life situations. You can have a MBA from Harvard Business School, but that will not automatically translate into profits until you develop the skill to apply that knowledge in a real business world. Many people have ended up frustrated and disappointed by the poor performance of a partner who had all the accolades but failed to deliver. Sometimes you might have to settle for someone with less accolades, but who is filled with wisdom.

6. Team player

Some people are just too into themselves that it's impossible for them to work with other people. When you partner with someone like this, you end up not accessing the benefits of partnership. Partnering with someone who can't value you, your ideas or your input is a total waste of time. Make sure you partner with someone who is humble, teachable, a good listener and a great student of life—a team player.

7. Track record of productivity

Accolades and degrees do not guarantee productivity either. I've made this mistake as a leader so many times. I've given someone an important position just based on their long resume and their enticing ability to sell themselves. Before getting a partner, you have to do your homework and inquire of this person's track record of productivity. If they've never produced anything where they are coming from, it's likely they won't produce anything for you. It's that simple. That does not mean you can't take a chance on someone who is completely new to the game. As long as they are honest with where they are, willing, and available, it's worth putting them on a trial period. Some of the best people who have worked for me did not show up with a huge record of accomplishments, but were simply hungry, passionate, teachable, and humble.

7 Ways to Maintain a Great Relationship with Your Partner

1. Mutual respect

You have to give honor and respect to your partner. Partnerships fail the moment one party begins to think they are better than the other. Just like any sports team, there will be seasons where a particular person is hot and delivering high results. A great team knows to support and appreciate each other through the dynamics of performance.

2. Honesty and transparency

Honesty builds trust. Without trust it's impossible to maintain a healthy partnership. You have to agree to have a "full disclosure" policy. One of the policies that made Steve Jobs and Apple successful is the "Fearless Feedback" principle. You have to be intentional about creating an atmosphere of transparency. This means that you have to be able to tell your partner the truth if you feel his or her idea is not good enough. It takes hard work and requires developing some communication skills. It also means that you have to develop a tough skin and not get sensitive every time your partner tells you your ideas are not good enough. It is in this honest dialog, clothed with respect, that great ideas are birthed.

3. Clear expectations

A lot of great partnerships have been cut short because expectations were not clear from the beginning. Be sure that you are clear on what your partner expects from you, and that you have clearly articulated what you expect from your partner. Mention every expectation whether significant or insignificant.

4. Growing together

Individual growth is determined by a set of experiences you go through over the years. Together, be sure to attend life transforming seminars or encounters that have power to alter your professional life. Otherwise, you will grow apart.

5. Friendship

There is nothing that connects people like friendship. Friendship automatically produces trust. You may not have all the time in the world to hangout after work hours, but the time you can invest playing golf or going hunting, or shopping and getting your nails done together can build a greater connection and produce synergy beyond what you can achieve in the conference room.

6. Intentional communication

You have to value communication enough to schedule it and make it a part of your work culture. You can never communicate enough. Create time to assess work, go over progress reports and set a new game plan. Silence causes people to imagine problems that don't exist, which in turn creates tension.

7. Mediation

You can and should expect conflict in every partnership. Conflict is not always a negative thing. There are some healthy conflicts and confrontations that are necessary and inevitable. There will be times where you just don't seem to agree. You have to call upon someone that you both respect who will come and mediate.

Key Questions
1. Who are the three most important partners in my life?
2. What are the three things I should do in order to keep them happy?
3. What three things should I do every week in order to grow our relationship?

Chapter 9

DELEGATION

Exodus 18:21
"But select capable men from all the people—men who fear
God, trustworthy men who hate dishonest gain—and appoint
them as officials over thousands, hundreds, fifties and tens."

This scripture is about an interesting scenario where Moses was receiving advice from his father-in-law to appoint delegates to help him lead the millions of children of Israel. At this point, Moses was doing all the leadership duties by himself: solving disputes, marrying people, conducting funerals, and more. He was the commander-in-chief as well as pastor. He was burning out quickly and was on the verge of a nervous breakdown. To rescue Moses from a leadership tragedy waiting to happen, his father-in-law came to him and said "appoint other leaders as officials over thousands, hundreds, fifties and tens."—Delegate!

3 Things Delegation did for Moses

1. Now Moses was only going to focus on decisions that affected millions, while the others would be in charge of decisions that affected thousands, hundreds, fifties and tens. Moses reduced his work load.
2. Moses would only focus his time and energy on the big decisions and issues that affected the whole nation while the others would deal with the lesser and more trivial matters like domestic issues and

resolving conflicts among the people. Moses was now able to prioritize and focus on the most important tasks first.

3. Moses made himself more effective by preserving himself from being over-worked.

The Dangers of Overload as a Leader

Over-loading yourself with too much work and doing unnecessary things stops acceleration and slows you down. This is the one thing that stops many from being as effective as they ought to be. Growing up in Africa, I remember many times being on an overloaded bus. In many developing countries they are not as strict with that stuff as the police are here in the West. I would be late for my appointments many times because these overloaded public vehicles moved slower than a turtle. Tragically, many times the buses would tip over, crush and kill many people. This is what happens when someone overloads their life with too many responsibilities and tasks. Not only does it slow you down greatly, but it could destroy and crush your whole vision. Delegation works in the opposite direction, it speeds you up!

Delegation Allows You to Focus on Your Priorities

Acts 6:1-4 "In those days when the number of disciples was increasing, the Grecian Jews among them complained against the Hebraic Jews because their widows were being overlooked in the daily distribution of food. So the Twelve gathered all the disciples together and said, 'It would not be right for us to neglect the ministry of the word of God in order to wait on tables. Brothers, choose seven men from among you who are known to be full of the Spirit and wisdom. We will turn this responsibility over to them and will give our attention to prayer and the ministry of the word.'"

In this scripture the disciples started neglecting the ministry of prayer and the reading of the Word (their number one priority) because they were busy distributing food and taking care of all the domestic duties. This was during a time where many people were getting converted and joining them, so all of a sudden the disciples had too many people and responsibilities to attend to. Acts 6 is the account of their realization to fix the problem through delegation. They decided to appoint seven men who would serve so they could focus on their priority of praying and reading the Word. The other danger of lack of delegation is neglecting the most important things. You lose focus and therefore become less effective. Delegation allows you to focus on your priorities.

5 Things that Delegation Does for You

1. Reduces your load so you can run fast. (That's why all the runners who compete in speed races, especially the 100 meter race, wear the lightest shoes they can find.)
2. Frees you from unnecessary things so you can focus on your priorities.
3. Preserves you from the setback caused by carrying extra-baggage. (We all know how expensive it is to pay for extra baggage at the airport.)
4. Gives you an opportunity to develop others around you into great leaders.
5. Gives other people around you an opportunity to exercise their gifts.

4 Ways to Recognize the Need for Delegation

1. When you are doing a task that someone else under you can do 60 percent as good as you or better.
2. Taking care of insignificant tasks while those under your leadership lay dormant.
3. Over-working yourself to a point where you are almost burning out.
4. Ignoring important tasks which cause you to appear careless.

7 Qualifications to Look at in Order to Locate a Good Delegate

1. Skilled

There is a tangible distinction when someone with years of training and experience work in their field of expertise. Though we should be open minded to training protégés and delegating work to them, you need skilled delegates in the key areas of your organization.

2. Servanthood spirit

A delegate is there to serve. If a delegate is un-teachable and reluctant to serve you fully, they will cause you to fall short on your responsibilities as a leader.

3. Responsible

The reason you delegate is to reduce the number of projects you are responsible over. If you delegate to someone who is skilled to do the work but is not responsible, then you have not delegated—you are still responsible.

4. Presentable

Your delegate's duty is to represent you, not him or herself. That's why you need a delegate who is intentional about being presentable. Your delegate is the messenger who carries your message. Your delegate is the packaging in which your product is served. Your delegate has the power to sell your product positively or negatively due to their presentation. Don't be afraid to set a standard of dressing and conduct with your delegates. They represent you and you are the one who would suffer the consequences.

5. Solutions provider

You need someone who is fast and creative—someone who always looks to provide solutions for you, not to present you with more problems. That's why they are there as a delegate in the first place.

6. Dedicated to your vision

You need someone who looks out for your best interest and is not concerned about promoting him or herself. Your message is compromised to your potential customers or market when there is division. As I previously mentioned, "Di" is an English prefix that stands for "two." It's where we get the word "dual" from (di-vision= two-visions). Having a laser focused vision is one of the greatest attributes to growth and acceleration. Even though your delegate may be one who wears many hats or may also be a visionary and a leader of their own enterprise, they have to be dedicated to your vision when they are on the job.

7. Track record of productivity

Like a great partner, a great delegate should have a track record of productivity, not talk alone.

5 Reasons People Fail to Delegate

1. Lack of trust

Many people fail because of fear that people will let them down or mess up their vision and project. You have to do your due diligence to examine a delegate before releasing authority and responsibility, but after that your trust in your delegate is the tool that empowers them to bring you high productivity. Don't micromanage.

2. Inability to teach

Take time to develop a skill to teach to others and raise up quality protégés. You might need to take a course or sit under the tutorage of others who know how to teach and develop protégés. It's these protégés who become your key delegates and later on the successors who sustain the lifeline of your vision. Every healthy organization should have a systematic developmental program in place.

3. Lack of patience

It's hard work to train people and requires a lot of patience. It's not pretty to train others. It's dirty work, but you have to roll up your sleeves and do the work. Be patient and willing to invest the time to train. Remember that each one of your delegates has different learning needs—there is no cookie cutter method.

4. Small vision mindset

Many people fail to delegate because they think it's easier, cheaper and quicker to just do the job themselves. What they don't realize is that by doing everything themselves they don't grow and become stuck doing the same old little jobs for the rest of their lives. This mindset causes stagnancy. Time is your most valuable commodity; spend it focusing on what's most profitable.

5. Failure to break unproductive cycles

Many of us are so used to doing something one way that it becomes a cycle. We have adopted most of these cycles from parents or the leaders we've grown up under. Some cycles are positive and some are not and need to be eradicated and replaced by new success-producing ones. Some cycles and habits may be great for someone else, but are simply outdated to facilitate the growth of your vision. One of these broken cycles is working without delegates.

Key Questions
1. Who are my three top delegates?
2. Who are the three people in my life who can help me more and become my delegates?
3. What are the three unnecessary tasks I'm doing that I should drop from my "to do" list?